Offensive in the Balkans

The Potential for a Wider War as a Result of Foreign Intervention in Bosnia-Herzegovina

BY YOSSEF BODANSKY

Dedicated to the Memory of
Emmanuel Shapiro
1928-1995.

Father-in-Law, Soul-Mate, and a Friend

Contents

	The States of the Former Yugoslavia (map)	6
	Turdjman's sketch for the partition of Bosnia	7
	Foreword	8
1.	Whither the Balkans?	10
2.	Origins	28
3.	Setting the Context	31
4.	Changing Europe	33
5.	Local Roots	37
6.	Sarajevo's Way	51
7.	The Outsiders	66
8.	The Bosnian *Jihad*	71
9.	Manipulating Washingon	82
10.	Between Belgrade and Zagreb	86
11.	The Summer of 1995	92
12.	Between Moscow and Berlin	102
13.	What Next?	106
14.	Lest We Forget the Former Yugoslavia	108
	Selected Bibliography	111
	About the Author	115

Offensive in the Balkans

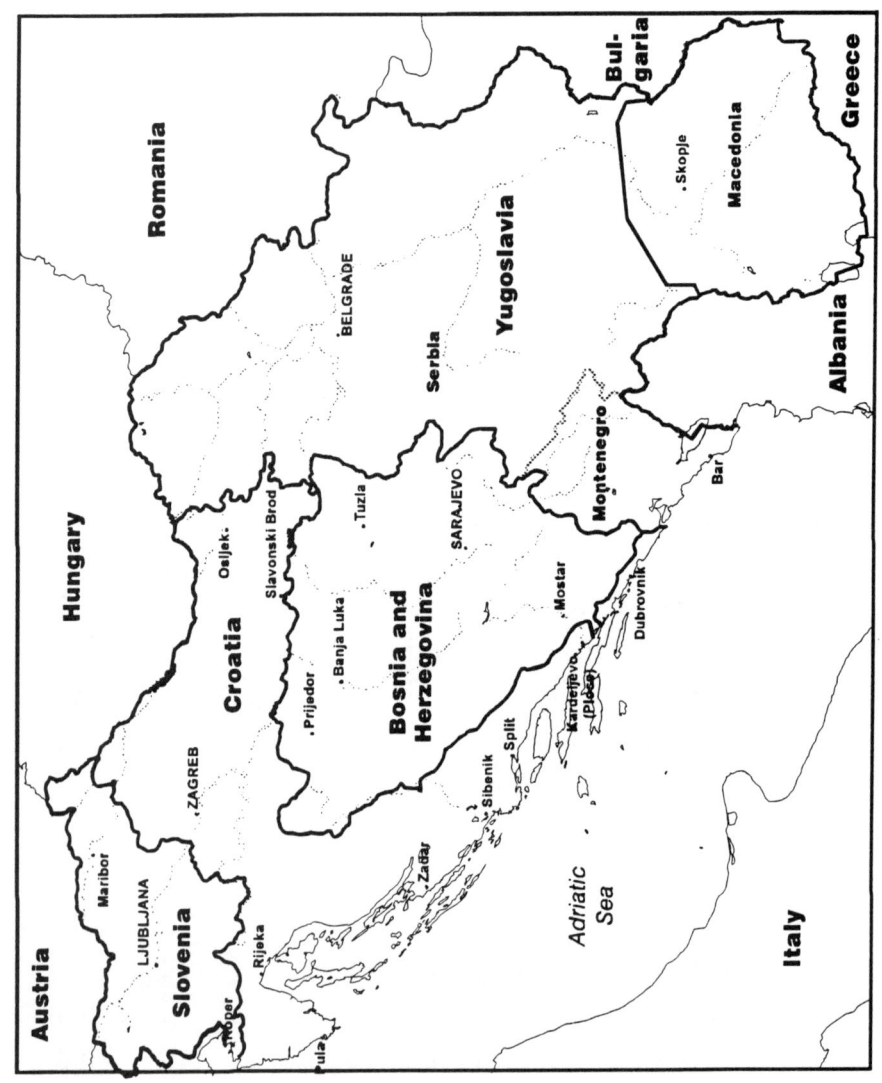

6.

Offensive in the Balkans

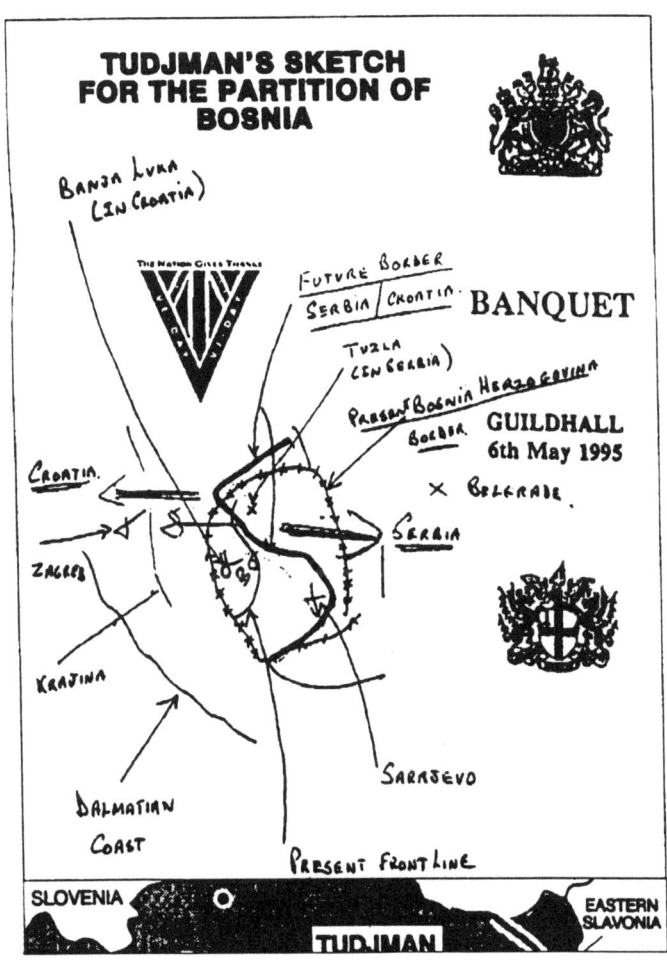

Croatian President Franjo Tudjman's map, drawn for a journalist at the official V-J (Victory Over Japan) day 50th anniversary celebration dinner in London on May 6, 1995, showing how he felt Bosnia-Herzegovina would in the future be divided between Croatia and Serbia. The map was reproduced in the August 7, 1995, edition of the London newspaper, **The Sunday Times.**

Foreword

The West has for so long lived with the illusion that the world was at peace following World War II that it now finds it difficult to comprehend the factors which lead to war. Wars were, however, an ongoing facet of life in much of the world during the post-World War II bi-polar nuclear stalemate, and it says much about the "sophisticated" societies of the West that they felt that the end of the Cold War would usher in an era of even greater peace in the world: a peace free of the tensions caused by the existence of two massively-armed and mutually hostile (albeit non-warring) nuclear camps.

It is exactly this "sophistry of naïvete", this deliberate refusal to learn from history, which has allowed some politicians in Washington DC and in Europe to bring about an escalation in the conflict in the former Yugoslavia during the 1990s. This situation has been abetted, if not caused, by a severe and emotional imbalance in both public media reporting *and* in intelligence reporting on the situation which has been underway in the Balkans since the beginning of the 1990s. Political populism will always follow emotional news media reporting, particularly in this age of instant television coverage.

The International Strategic Studies Association (ISSA) has always striven to ensure that policymakers around the world base their leadership on firm foundations of facts, historical and geopolitical understanding, and an inherent understanding of cultures. We felt, as a result of the worsening situation in the Balkans and the clear prospect that the conflict there could develop into a new World War, that ISSA had an obligation to publish this extensively-researched book by our Director of Research, Yossef Bodansky.

We will continue to support the publication of a more balanced analysis of the conflict in the Balkans (as we will on other crisis situations) as part of our ongoing effort to ensure that policymakers can have an alternative basis of reasoning for their actions and avoid dependence on current reporting which fails to give the historical and global context for the crisis.

This book contains information and analysis which will not be widely seen in other publications, and we urge its urgent consideration if a wider crisis is to be averted.

— Gregory R. Copley,
President,
The International Strategic Studies Association,
Alexandria, Virginia: November 1995

1. Whither the Balkans?

The US Clinton Administration, exploiting public shock and outrage over macabre television images of carnage caused by an explosion on Market Street in Sarajevo on August 28, 1995, moved quickly to substantially alter the character of US involvement in the war in the former Yugoslavia. Even though sizable elements of the US Armed Forces were committed to combat — the US provided the bulk of aircrews used over Bosnia-Herzegovina — neither the US Congress, nor the US public were informed about the change in policy. On the contrary, there was initially a concentrated effort to conceal the extent of the change in US commitment.

After blaming the Bosnian Serbs "beyond reasonable doubt" for the "mortar shell" which caused the Market Street carnage, the Clinton Administration then used this incident to justify the massive bombing campaign which was launched against the Bosnian Serbs virtually immediately. On August 29, President Clinton called the still-escalating bombing campaign "an appropriate response to the shelling of Sarajevo". Starting in the pre-dawn hours of August 30, wave after wave of NATO aircraft — 80 to 85 percent of them US — began pounding Bosnian Serb strategic and regular military objectives. Initial targets were around Sarajevo, giving credence to the fig-leaf claim of retaliation for the "mortar shell". But, within a few hours, bombing raids were taking place all over Bosnia-Herzegovina.

Thus, rhetoric aside, the US became an active and dominant participant in the wars in the former Yugoslavia.

It was only after the first waves of predominantly US NATO strike aircraft had already dropped their bombs over Bosnian Serb targets that the Clinton Administration grudgingly began to tell truth. By this time, wide cracks were beginning to appear in the claim that the "mortar shell" had been fired by the Bosnian Serbs.

At first, the United Nations Protection Force (UNPRO-FOR) acknowledged that the widespread bombing was not a retaliation for this specific mortar shell but rather an humanitarian operation aimed at protecting the civilian population of Sarajevo from the Serb gunners. "The aim of the operation is to remove the threat of heavy weapons around Sarajevo," said UN spokesman Lt.-Col. Chris Vernon.

By now, however, the bombing raids were expanded to include Serb positions overlooking the towns of Tuzla and Gorazde. These bombings were presented as defending the Bosnian Muslim "safe havens" within these towns from possible future attacks or retaliation by the Bosnian Serb forces. "We hope that this operation will also demonstrate to the Bosnian Serbs the futility of further military actions," said an August 29 statement released in Brussels by North Atlantic Treaty Organization (NATO) Secretary-General Willy Claes.

It was only when the US aircraft began bombing Bosnian Serb positions overlooking the town of Mostar, in south-west Bosnia-Herzegovina, that the truth finally began to emerge. Mostar has never been a "safe haven". The local Bosnian Serb forces had remained quiet for several months while overlooking the Croat forces slaughtering the Bosnian Muslims in Mostar: their brothers in the US-brokered federation. Mostar is also the place where key Croat forces are now being built up for an offensive push on Banja Luka. And these Croat forces might need some help breaking through the Serbian defensive positions one of these days.

On September 8, the same day a breakthrough was reached

in the peace negotiations in Geneva, US military officials said "the bombing campaign could shift to a new set of targets in the north-western of the country", particularly the Serb military infrastructure in the Banja Luka area. No effort was made by US officials to explain the connection between these new objectives and the safety of Sarajevo or even other "safe havens". On the other hand, the presence of important Bosnian Serb strategic targets was stressed.

The real objective of the bombing clearly had nothing to do with the "mortar shell", or the safety of the Bosnian Muslim safe havens. The US is intervening in the wars in Bosnia-Herzegovina in order to deprive the Bosnian Serbs of a military victory and compel them to acquiesce to a decidedly discriminatory political solution. "The Bosnian Serbs, especially after the events of the last 12 hours, ought to have concluded that there is no military victory in sight for them, the tide of the war has turned against them, their dream of a greater Serbia is no more, it's time to face the responsibility of peace," US State Department spokesman Nicholas Burns said on August 30, 1995. Similarly, Assistant Secretary of State Richard Holbrooke welcomed the NATO air strikes as a long-awaited sign that Bosnia is "moving toward peace".

Washington's closest allies were alarmed by the emerging objectives of the bombing campaign: a campaign in which their own aircraft and ground forces were taking an active part under US NATO commanders. London's reaction was the strongest. On August 30, a British official shied away from the superlatives uttered by the US spokesmen. "The objective of this action is not to bomb the Bosnian Serbs to the negotiating table. We're not there to fight a war," he stressed. He explained that London vowed to continue participation in the NATO actions "until Sarajevo was safe from hostile gunfire" but stressed that the UN had no mandate for, and the British Government is against, "blasting the Bosnian Serbs into submission".

The Clinton Administration remained unwavering on the path it had chosen. Claiming to be committed to finding a peaceful solution to the wars in Bosnia-Herzegovina, the Clinton Administration has actually been committed to forcing a Muslim victory on the entire Bosnia-Herzegovina. The essence of this victory is empowering the Islamist Sarajevo leadership which, at the very best, enjoys around 20 percent support and recognition in a country where more than two-thirds of the population is Christian and adamantly opposed to living in the Muslim state. Some 30 to 35 percent of the Bosnians are Muslims, and at least one-third of them support the moderate Islamic group around the leadership of Abdić, so that even if all other Bosnian Muslims support the Sarajevo regime they would still constitute only 20 percent of the population.

Since mid-Summer, US negotiators have been creating the impression of being serious about pursuing a just peace and an even-handed diplomatic process. It was the lure of the Clinton Administration's trying to confront the grim realities in the former Yugoslavia which made Serbian President Slobodan Milošević betray the Krajina Serbs, and the sacred tenet of Serb unity, in the name of a US peace proposal. Belgrade hoped that the profound sacrifice of the Serbs would be appreciated and that their desire for a settlement of the war would be finally accepted.

Belgrade made a major mistake. Starting the third week of August, the Clinton Administration sharply deviated from the impression of sincerity impressed upon both Zagreb and Belgrade, and instead endorsed Izetbegović's "12-Point" peace plan which had been submitted in mid-August 1995. Sarajevo's peace plan set pre-conditions known to be unacceptable to the Serbs. Sarajevo insists not only that any peace must be based on Bosnia's sovereignty and territorial integrity, but that no population group would be permitted to secede from Bosnia-Herzegovina and join a neighboring country. Sarajevo also insists that the 1994 Contact Group Peace plan, particularly the maps already rejected by the Serbs, should remain the sole basis for any settlement.

Significantly, Sarajevo insisted on the de-ligitimization of the

Bosnian Serb leadership. Calling the Pale leaders "war criminals", Sarajevo insists on their persecution and says that no negotiations will be held with them. This point was quickly and publicly endorsed by Holbrooke, thus raising doubt about his ability to serve as a mediator.

In order to stress the Islamic character of the future Bosnia-Herzegovina, Sarajevo has insisted since early Summer 1995 that any peace plan must be signed by a representative of the Organization of Islamic Conference (OIC) in addition to the members of the Contact Group and the UN. This issue is also one of Izetbegović's 12-Point peace plan endorsed by Holbrooke. Thus, while the US continues to point to the "multi-national character" of a future Bosnia-Herzegovina, Washington moved quickly to appease Sarajevo on this point. On August 30, the Contact Group announced formal briefings given to Islamic Ambassadors in Geneva — representing the OIC — on the peace process in the former Yugoslavia. Diplomats in Geneva stressed that the two main issues which the OIC was to be briefed on were the current US proposals for a Bosnian settlement and the additional military threats and incentives.

The ensuing events in Bosnia-Herzegovina, as well as the entire former Yugoslavia, cannot be comprehended except in the context of the state of mind of the upper echelons of the Bosnian Muslim leadership in Sarajevo, and, in all likelihood, the key US officials dealing with the region.

By now, mid-August, Sarajevo had concluded that the US initiative in its original form was doomed, an opinion shared by local diplomats. "The Bosnian Government will reject the peace plan. I don't think the Americans will get them around," observed a senior West European diplomat in Sarajevo. "They [the Bosnian Muslims] don't trust anyone except for themselves." The Bosnian Muslim leadership was in a combative mood. On August 13, Izetbegović vowed that "Sarajevo, of course with the help of God and our efforts, will be unblocked by political or military means. We must not enter Winter in this situation, and we will not." Sarajevo was convinced that a military solution was the only viable option, and that a Bosnian Muslim victory could only be made possible by a massive US-led bombing. This issue was raised in the negotiations with Ambassador Holbrooke. The Bosnian Muslim leadership was convinced that Washington supported their position. On August 16, Foreign Minister Muhamed Sacirbegović stressed that his recent talks with Holbrooke focused "on what needs to be done to compel the Serbian side to accept the plan, and how in fact will the Bosnian Government and its armed forces be provided the opportunity to resist aggression."

Little wonder that Sarajevo was now convinced that the Clinton Administration was favorably disposed toward a marked escalation of the US/NATO military involvement in Bosnia-Herzegovina — in the form of massive bombing of Bosnian Serb objectives — thus facilitating a Bosnian Muslim military victory. The upper echelons in Sarajevo were under the impression that the Clinton Administration only needed a legitimate excuse in order to launch the massive air campaign. Therefore, the Bosnian Muslims prepared a self-inflicted atrocity to be blamed on the Serbs, thus serving as the excuse which Washington needed.

According to a top Russian military intelligence officer, they "learned about the [Bosnian Muslim] plan to stage the explosion yet on August 20". Russian intelligence briefed the US, German and Croat "leaderships" fearing an uncontrolled escalation. However, the top officer explained, "they did nothing to cut short the provocation and kept silent about the information", convincing Moscow that it was in their interest to see the provocation happen.

Meanwhile, Sarajevo was busy preparing the diplomatic and media grounds for a dramatic collapse of the peace negotiations and the resumption of hostilities. Indeed, starting the second half of August 1995, Sarajevo was raising the pressure on the Clinton Administration to further increase the pressure on the Serbs. While in Washington on August 23, Sarajevo's Foreign Minister Muhamed Sacirbey [Sacirbegović's Westernized name] issued an ultimatum to Washington. He told Secretary of State Warren Christopher that Sarajevo would give the US initiative only two months to make progress. If nothing tangible happened, the Bosnian Muslims would commit themselves to a military solution to the conflict.

By now, the Clinton Administration was convinced that the Serbs — both Pale and Belgrade — would never accept the Holbrooke version of the Izetbegović plan. The US expected, and West European governments were so briefed, that the Serbs would reject the offered plan, thus clearing the way for the sought-after military escalation. To further reduce the likelihood of Pale accepting the peace initiative Holbrooke publicly deligitimized Pale Government. He insisted that the Bosnian Serbs leaders were "war criminals" whom the US could not trust nor with whom they could negotiate. On August 27, Holbrooke introduced additional pressure on the Serbs. "If this peace initiative does not get moving, dramatically moving in the next week or two, the consequences will be very adverse to the Serbian goals," Holbrooke warned.

And then, the US policy faced an unforeseen calamity: both Pale and Belgrade agreed to the US conditions. Serb leaders authoritatively announced, and on time, their commitment to further negotiating in accordance with the US peace plan.

Thus, on August 28, at the beginning of a fateful week, Izetbegović and the Sarajevo leadership were in Paris for a summit originally planned to sanctify the US-led NATO military escalation against the Serbs in response to their anticipated rejection of the Peace Plan. But the Serbs only reiterated their commitment to negotiate, and, since the Clinton Administration would not listen to them, also formally notified former President Jimmy Carter and others to make sure the word got to Washington DC. The Clinton Administration was suddenly faced with the dreaded possibility that they would have to negotiate with the Serbs on substance.

And then the ubiquitous "Serb mortar shell" exploded on Market Street, killing nearly 40 civilians. Not only was the shell's timing perfect, but a professional camera crew was ready and on-hand to record the scene in all its gore even before the emergency services began arriving. Although the UN rushed to determine "beyond reasonable doubt" that the 120mm mortar shell came from Bosnian Serb positions south of Sarajevo, many major forensic questions remained unanswered.

Col. Andrei Demurenko, a Russian artillery officer who is the Chief of Staff for the Sarajevo sector of the United Nations Peacekeeping mission in Bosnia, formally stated that "technical analysis shows that a 120mm mortar bomb which killed 37 people and wounded 85 on Monday could not have come from Bosnian Serb Army positions". A Canadian military expert pointed to "anomalies with the fuse" which, to his expert opinion, suggested that both fuse and shell "had not come from a mortar tube at all".

The British ammunition experts and French military analysts with UNPROFOR who examined the crater a mere 40 minutes after the explosion not only found no evidence that the Bosnian Serbs had fired the mortar shell, but concluded that the forensic evidence pointed to the Bosnian Muslim army as being responsible for the shelling. However, these finding were rejected by a senior US officer with UNPROFOR. Citing the presence of a "fuse furrow" — a distinct small groove left on the surface when the fuse first hit the ground that the British and French experts insist did not exist at the crater site — this US senior officer overruled the British-French report and instead pushed through UN channels his own report blaming the Bosnian Serbs for the shell.

This was not the first time the excuse of a "Serb mortar shell" was used to impose a drastic change in the military situation in Bosnia-Herzegovina. Indeed, UN officials in Sarajevo described the August 28 shell as "an almost carbon copy of the shelling 18 months ago". Then the UN safe area policy was enacted and persisted even as the February 1994 explosion in the Sarajevo Market was eventually found out to be a self-inflicted act of terrorism by the Sarajevo regime. The UN officials stressed the similarity between the two events as catalysts for a US-pushed drastic change in NATO and UN policy and military actions in favor of the Bosnian Muslims.

The swift determination of Serb culpability came even though there is a long record of Muslim self-inflicted terrorism and sniper fire since 1992, acknowledged by senior UN officials, UNPROFOR senior officers, French and British military investigation teams, and other experts. However, all the confirmations and acknowledgments of the self-inflicted terrorism by Sarajevo came after lengthy and thorough investigations, long after the shocking and emotional impact of the carnage had already been fully exploited against the Serbs. Moreover, being "old news" and politically "incorrect", these findings were hardly ever reported by the Western media.

Nor was the Clinton Administration even a little suspicious that the latest carnage came perfectly timed for Sarajevo's political strategy. The "mortar shell" exploded exactly at the time when the Europeans had been pressing Washington to be more even-handed in its approach to finding a solution to the Bosnian crisis. The Serbs were publicly demonized anew just when Izetbegović was coming up with a peace plan which was essentially a non-negotiable ultimatum, and which the US was racing to embrace while the UK and France were adamantly opposed to such a one-sided approach. In late August 1995, the conventional opinion in Western Europe was that whatever the Bosnian Serb reaction to the inevitable NATO retaliation would be, it would in effect paralyze the diplomatic process and revive the primacy of the military option. This is presently Sarajevo's preferred approach.

But all the lingering questions and doubts — both military and political — were quickly cast aside under US pressure so that they did not interfere with the swift political capitalizing on the "Serb shell". Now, the Clinton Administration had both the fig leaf and excuse for the sought-after fundamental change of US policy. Within a few hours, the US pushed NATO onto a marked escalation of direct military involvement which, if not contained, might well lead the US into a war in the Balkans.

And so, in the pre-dawn hours of August 30, 1995, a massive bombing and shelling campaign began. The strategic impact of this bombing campaign will not disappear. Irrespective of the amount of casualties and damage inflicted, the chances of a Sarajevo/Washington-style peace being accepted are even more remote. The willingness of the Serb leadership in both Belgrade and Pale to continue and talk with the US delegation, including making a major concession by agreeing to a single Serb delegation — thus in effect self-deligitimizing the Bosnian Serb leadership, long a major objective of Sarajevo and Washington — should not be taken out of proportion. The Serbs still have legitimate and vital interests which are incompatible with the peace plan of Washington or Sarajevo. Moreover, the Clinton Administration is eroding its own credibility as a peacemaker by increasingly justifying the widening bombing campaign by the need "to punish the Serbs", and by pushing the UN/NATO to issue additional ultimatums to the Serbs, such as lifting the siege on Sarajevo, under the threat of renewed and expanded bombings.

While the Clinton Administration espouses the contribution of the latest bombing campaign to the peace process, its closest allies — the Sarajevo leadership — actively prepares for the expansion and escalation of the war in Bosnia-Herzegovina by capitalizing on the impact of the bombing campaign. The Bosnian Muslim leadership is emboldened by the strikes and the international pressure on the Serbs. Sarajevo is increasingly suspicious about their Croat "allies". Sarajevo is therefore determined to exploit the outcome of the punitive bombing to improve its military posture against both Serbs and Croats. Military and militant leaders are convinced that only a major decisive military victory will enable the Bosnian Muslims to consolidate control over the entire Bosnia-Herzegovina.

General Rasim Delić, the Commander of the Bosnian Muslim army, has repeated this argument ever since the NATO bombing campaign began. On August 28, just after the "Serb

Shell" exploded, Delić, as well as the rest of the Sarajevo leadership, began demanding a marked escalation of NATO retaliation. Delić dismissed the US peace initiative or any other non-military outcome of the bombing. "We have only one direction, and that is to continue fighting," he explained. Delić stressed Sarajevo's commitment to "liberating all Bosnian territory" by force of arms.

As the bombing campaign began to unfold, Zagreb became convinced that it was imperative to capitalize on the effect of the bombing to seize the military initiative on the ground. The August 30, 1995, clarifications by a Western diplomat in Zagreb that the goal of the bombings was to "deliver a political message and not to change the overall balance of power", were openly ridiculed.

Croatian senior military officials and analysts described the initial effect of the NATO bombing as "a major shift in military might to the advantage of the Muslim-Croat alliance". Several experts predicted that a correct capitalization on the effect of the bombing could finally create conditions for victory over the Serbs. "We are talking about a strategic turning point where Bosnian army and Croat troops seriously outnumber the Serbs in every respect," explained Fran Visnar, a Croat military expert. "This action will give wings to the Bosnian and Croat troops, especially in western Bosnia where the Serbs are most vulnerable since they have no friendly border."

Croatian military analysts expected the Bosnian Muslim and Croat forces to capitalize on NATO's destruction of Serb guns around Sarajevo in order to try to lift the siege of the city by force of arms. The Croat experts expect an attack from the south, where the Serb ring is the thinnest, from Mount Igman through the airport towards the city. "NATO warned the warring parties not to take advantage of the strikes for military gain, but the fact is that the present situation has created ripe conditions for piercing the blockade," declared Karl Gorinsek, a Croat military expert. The US bombing in the Mostar and Banja Luka areas would only expedite such offensives.

By mid-September 1995, the US and NATO bombing continued to expand, now including both additional objectives and what NATO called Option Two targets: mainly ammunition dumps and radar stations. The US also escalated its campaign, firing cruise missiles at Bosnian Serb strategic facilities in Banja Luka in western Bosnia-Herzegovina, objectives which have nothing to do with Sarajevo but were key to neutralizing the air defenses of the Serbs in anticipation of further escalation of the fighting. NATO was, by mid-September, getting ready to bomb Option Three targets, which include power plants, airports, roads, bridges, fuel supplies and other strategic installations. A Pentagon official admitted that the planned escalation in the air campaign was a "quantum leap" which made NATO "nervous".

The representatives of the three warring parties had signed off in Geneva, back on September 8, on the one-page agreement on basic principles for diplomatic negotiations to conclude the war. They reaffirmed the basis for the territorial split to be based on the long-standing division of 49 percent of Bosnia-Herzegovina to the Serbs and 51 percent to the existing federation of Bosnian Muslims and Croats. The agreement also stipulated that each of the ethnic entities has the right to establish "special relationships" with neighboring countries; essentially permitting the Serbs to develop the same type of relations currently existing between the Croats of Bosnia-Herzegovina and the Croats of Croatia.

In Belgrade, the Serbs also signed an agreement to evacuate their heavy weapons from the Sarajevo area in the presence of US diplomat Richard Holbrooke. Implementation began quickly and progressed at a varying pace. The Sarajevo airport opened, and the Bosnian Serbs even promised to restore some of the services to Sarajevo. Consequently, NATO put a hold on its air strikes.

By now, however, Zagreb was capitalizing on the damage to, and demoralization of, the Bosnian Serb forces. On September 11, 1995, Croat regular forces already on Bosnia-Herzegovina soil supported by additional Croatian Army forces from Croatia (Krajina area), launched a sustained and massive offensive on Bosnian Serb forces in western Bosnia-Herzegovina. They did not even try to conceal themselves under a claim of being "Bosnian Croat forces". They were in Bosnia-Herzegovina in clear violation of the United Nations prohibition on the entry of Yugoslav or Croatian forces into Bosnia-Herzegovina, but nothing was said by the media or by the UN. They were supported on the September 11 offensive by a few Bosnian Muslim token units.

Within a week, the Croats were close to a final assault on Banja Luka, when they stopped under US pressure.

It was a well-prepared offensive which came in the aftermath of lengthy deployment of forces and complex coordination of multiple axes of advance. The September offensive had the same characteristics of the Croat assault on the Krajina a few months before. Considering the intimate relations of the Croat Armed Forces with their US instructors and Washington (to be discussed later in this book), including the preparations for the assault on the Krajina, it is inconceivable that these elaborate preparations had not been known by Washington. Moreover, considering that the Croatian *blitzkrieg* in the Krajina saw massive use of close air support from MiG-21s and Mi-24s, the US destruction of the Bosnian Serb air defense in Banja Luka made perfect sense.

There are reasons to believe that the Croatian and Bosnian Muslim preparations for the offensive were conducted in concert with earlier US (under NATO banner) preparations for the air campaign: a campaign which was unleashed as a response to the "Serb mortar shell".

Significantly, at least until early September, analysts in the Pentagon were convinced that a diplomatic solution involving the 49:51 division of Bosnia-Herzegovina was "unworkable" because the Bosnian Serbs, then holding 70 percent of Bosnia-Herzegovina, would not surrender the land without a major military defeat. The Clinton Administration was determined to deliver such a defeat and was thus most likely to tacitly assist the Croats and Bosnian Muslims in their preparations for the military option.

Zagreb, which knew perfectly well that Pale had already accepted the 49:51 division in principle but did not bother to correct Washington, had a different objective in the forthcoming escalation. Zagreb intended to make a major effort to capture Banja Luka in order to draw Belgrade into the war: still a major strategic objective of Zagreb.

In mid-September 1995, however, as the Croat-led offensive unfolded, the Bosnian Serb forces simply withdrew without major resistance and Belgrade did not show any indication that it would intervene. The Serbian leadership in both Belgrade and Pale must have realized that there was no point in fighting for areas which they would have to surrender anyway under political arrangements. "Mladic seems to be recognizing political reality," a UN official in Sarajevo explained, "and is not willing to fight for land that is inevitably going to be given up anyway." Thus, by the end of September, as the defense lines stabilized, the Bosnian Serbs controlled only about 55 percent of B-H, while the Muslims and Croats controlled 45 percent. The Croatian Armed Forces were the dominant military force facing the Serbs as Sarajevo was still urging a military escalation. New fighting was initiated by Bosnian Muslim forces in the vital Brcko corridor.

Late September and early October 1995 saw a race to consolidate ceasefire lines in Bosnia-Herzegovina, a pre-condition to the resumption of negotiations on a peaceful diplomatic settlement of the war.

From the very beginning of this phase, Sarajevo's real objectives differed from the declared position of the diplomatic process. By late September, Western diplomats and UN officials in Sarajevo were apprehensive about the true intentions and policies of the Bosnian Muslim Government. For example, in an off-the-record meeting between leading European diplomats and UN officials in Sarajevo on September 26, the participants worried out-loud about the implications and ramifications of the position of the Bosnian Muslim Government. A commonly-shared perception, in the words of one participating diplomat, was that Sarajevo "is trying to win at the negotiating table what it lost on the battlefield over 41 months of war".

"Forget the 51:49 territorial split which the [Izetbegović] Government agreed to," opined another diplomat. Sarajevo "is using the peace talks to insist on conditions to effectively deny the Serbs real autonomy, let alone the separate state they fought for. The constitutional guarantees the government is demanding would emasculate Serb nationalists on their 49 percent."

"The [Izetbegović] government's strategy is to drive a stake through the heart of the Serb Republic using democracy and human rights as the mallets," explained a UN official. "Not surprisingly, the Bosnian Serbs are having none of it."

A new cycle of fighting erupted on October 3, 1995. At first, Bosnian Muslim forces opened artillery fire on Serb position south-east of Sarajevo, particularly in the Trnovo area. This outbreak of fighting was most significant because, in support of the Trnovo operation, the Bosnian Muslim forces began firing heavy weapons from inside the 20km (12.5 mile) heavy weapons exclusion zone around Sarajevo. Only in September had Sarajevo committed itself not to use weapons in the exclusion zone as part of the deal which brought the Bosnian Serbs to withdraw their own heavy weapons from the zone.

But this was no mere violation of yet another agreement with UNPROFOR. Trnovo is the key to re-opening the road to Gorazde, and, had the Bosnian Serbs reacted to the Bosnian Muslim provocation and then most likely elicited a "retaliatory" NATO air strike, the Bosnian Muslim forces could have exploited the strike to break through the Serb lines and break the siege on Gorazde. As it was, the Bosnian Muslim provocative shelling was done in full view of UNPROFOR observers and, the moment the Bosnian Serb forces did not return fire, UNPROFOR had no alternative but to denounce Sarajevo.

Meanwhile, intense fighting flared up anew in north-west Bosnia-Herzegovina, with predominantly regular Croat forces (HV) resuming their advance into Bosnia-Herzegovina in order to consolidate strategic positions from where they would be able to launch a major offensive on Banja Luka.

These advances were first balanced by a series of localized counter-offensives by the Bosnian Serb forces. The Bosnian Serbs made substantial gains in the first days of October, and even threatened the Croat hold over key strategic cities. The Bosnian Serb counter-offensive prevented the Croats from consolidating their launching positions for a future offensive. However, after a few days the Bosnian Serbs lost momentum and their forces bogged down.

It was also in early October 1995 that some 3,500 Croat regular forces (HV) crossed into Bosnia-Herzegovina, advanced into the Bihać area and took positions in preparation for an offensive on Banja Luka from the west. On October 6, the UN confirmed the presence of 400 HV troops with heavy weapons facing key Serb positions in the area.

As the ceasefire date of October 10 was agreed upon, fighting intensified with all warring sides trying to grab last-minute gains and improve positions. Fighting escalated on October 8, with Croat reinforcements backed by heavy artillery and rocket launchers as well as Mi-24 helicopter gunships increasing the push along the entire front. A few Bosnian Serb air strikes failed to slow the Croat forces. There was also a surge in ethnic cleansing, primarily that of over 100,000 Serbs thrown out of local towns and villages seized by the Croats and Bosnian Muslim forces.

As the ceasefire hour was nearing, the Croat and a few Bosnian Muslim forces were gaining momentum in their offensives. So Sarajevo came up with a host of excuses why it was imperative to postpone the ceasefire. This maneuver, which was tacitly supported by the Clinton Administration, bought the Croat and Bosnian Muslim forces additional time to continue the offensive and improve their positions.

The Croat offensive culminated on October 11 with the HV (specifically, the Split-based 4th Brigade) completing the capture of a strategic road in the northwest of Bosnia-Herzegovina. This axis is a crucial strategic asset in a future offensive on Banja Luka and into Serbia proper. Regular Croat forces with token presence of Bosnian Muslim forces — mainly the 5th Corps in the Bihać area — were now deployed along a solid front, at times a mere 30kms (18 miles) from Banja Luka. "After the latest successes, conditions have been created for the final liberation of the Bosnian towns of Prijedor and Banja Luka," the 5th Corps announced. The HV's most forward position is the hydroelectric plant of Bocac on the River Vrbas, 25 km (15 miles) from Banja Luka.

The Bosnian Muslim forces already have a specific contingency plan for the completion of the occupation of western and northern Bosnia-Herzegovina. In early October, General Atif Dudaković, the commander of the 5th Corps, explained that the ultimate objective of the joint offensive with the HV was Banja Luka. He predicted that the "liberation of the Banja Luka Serbian stronghold is inevitable", and that the 5th Corps "will then continue to advance toward Breko and Bijeljina". Dudaković added that the capture of Banja Luka would be a pincer assault with the 7th Corps under the command of General Mehmed Alagić advancing from central Bosnia-Herzegovina.

Nevertheless, a new 60-day ceasefire was set for one minute after midnight on October 12, 1995 (local time). It seemed to be holding in the first hours. Sarajevo's acceptance of the ceasefire was conditional. Izetbegović stressed that the Bosnian Muslim forces "will cease all military activities except defensive ones as of midnight tonight". Specific orders qualifying defensive conditions had already been issued by Rasim Delić on Izetbegović's instructions. Significantly, Dudaković clarified Sarajevo's understanding of the ceasefire regime: "As long as peace agreement is not reached and signed, we do not feel obliged to implement a ceasefire." Indeed, Sarajevo accused the Bosnian Serbs of a major offensive along the key axis leading in the direction of Banja Luka within a few hours after the ceasefire went into effect. Defending against this alleged offensive could enable the 5th Corps to resume its advance.

Thus, the Bosnian crisis is far from over, and the massive bombing complicated an already complex situation. The challenge of resolving the convoluted crisis in the former Yugoslavia is growing. And so is the likelihood of a major military escalation which might well spread beyond the confines of the former Yugoslavia into the Balkans and all over Europe. It is therefore imperative to comprehend the roots, dynamics and scope of this crisis and intense war.

It is in the strategic context of the war that one can see how misguided the Clinton Administration's Bosnian policy really is. And if the crisis in the former Yugoslavia continues to evolve in its present course, the ensuing developments will be detrimental to the US' own national interest and national security.

2. Origins

Between June 5 and 28, 1389, on the Field of Blackbirds, now known as Kosovo, the rebelling forces of Serbia were soundly defeated by the advancing Turkish armies of the Sultan Murad I. Murad I himself was assassinated in Kosovo soon after the first battle. His son, who became the Sultan Bayazid, was also with the Turkish armies in the Balkans. He immediately ordered the execution of the captive King Lazar of Serbia as a blood revenge. Meanwhile, the Turkish armies intensified their assault on the remaining Serbian forces. Consequently, by June 28, 1389, the land of the Yugo [southern] Slavs was completely occupied by the Muslim Turks, and the centuries-long struggle of the southern Slavs, led by the Serbs, for independence and self-determination had just begun.

Since 1389, June 28 is known as *Vidovdan* — the Day When We Shall See — and is a national symbol of the Serbian defiant struggle for independence and self-determination against overwhelming odds and in a hostile world.

On June 28, 1989, the 600th anniversary of the sacred Battle of Kosovo, Slobodan Milošević, then an aspiring leader in the Yugoslav Republic of Serbia, delivered a speech at the monument for the Battle of Kosovo in Prishtina. Flanked by the other leaders of Federal Yugoslavia and its various national republics in what was supposed to be a commemoration of a joint historic milestone of all southern Slavs, Milošević spoke about the need to resurrect the glory and predominance of the Serbs. His was a measured and calm speech, logically outlining a vision of a Serbia moving to assume a greater and ultimately leading rôle in a united Yugoslavia.

Forthcoming as he was, Milošević had no illusion as to the fears his speech was causing among wide segments of Yugoslavia's multinational population. In their quest for a greater rôle in Yugoslavia, Milošević explained, the Serbs were facing a challenge of historical proportions: comparable to the historic Battle of Kosovo. "Six centuries [after Kosovo]," he told a huge, predominantly Serbian, audience, "we are again engaged in battles and quarrels. They are not armed battles, but this cannot be excluded yet." Milošević's prophesy of a new Balkan war, trials and tribulations, would be realized faster than anybody could dream on that fateful day in 1989.

In this demonstration of Serbian spirited nationalism, Milošević daringly brought to the open a fundamental process already taking place in Yugoslavia since 1986-87. It was the rapid erosion of the two socio-political taboos introduced by Tito and preserved by his heirs, namely, preventing at all cost: (1) the display of overt nationalism, and (2) the active participation of the masses in politics.

However, Milošević was not the first to raise these issues. The first cracks in these taboos had already been caused by the revival of Croatian nationalism as a political ideology in the late 1980s. This campaign was spearheaded by Franjo Tudjman, a former JNA [Yugoslav National Army] political general turned historian. Tudjman was legitimizing a lengthy underground struggle waged by Croatian nationalists, a struggle which included resorting to international terrorism. By the late 1980s, it did not take long for the same sentiments to lead to the rise of Slovenian nationalism. The explosive potential in Tudjman's ideological line was in the consequent insensitivity, hostility toward, and ultimately discrimination against, the Serbian population in Croatia and Slovenia. The emerging Croat and

Slovenian nationalist leaderships were fully aware of the ramifications of their ideological lines considering the increasingly confrontational attitudes they assumed toward the Serbs, both those living in their midst, and Serbia as a nation.

However, unlike the Serbs, whose revitalized quest for national self-identity went little beyond virulent rhetoric, the Croats began actively preparing for a unilateral secession by force of arms if necessary. The nationalist leadership was fully aware of the gravity of the decision they made, and therefore sought the patronage of foreign powers. In 1988, Tudjman made a secret visit to Germany, Croatia's patron in World War II. There, he met with Chancellor Helmut Kohl and other senior officials in order to formulate a joint policy to dismember Yugoslavia and establish a new independent Croatia. One of the first steps taken in accordance with these plans was to begin large-scale clandestine weapons acquisition in order to enable the Croats and Slovenes to launch their unilateral independence movement with armed militias. Meanwhile, the growing self-confidence of the Croat and Slovene nationalist leaderships was manifesting itself in mounting populist chauvinism and hostility toward Serbs.

Little wonder, therefore, that the mounting anti-Serb sentiments in Croatia and Slovenia since the late 1980s resulted in a backlash in Serbia where Milošević, a Stalinist turned populist, took the process one step further, into overt populism as seen in Kosovo in June 1989. It was becoming clear that Serbs, Croats and Slovenes were asserting their national self-awakening in a confrontational and hostile manner toward the other key nations of Yugoslavia. The ensuing populist response to the new nationalistic winds made it clear that a violent eruption was all but inevitable. Thus, although neither side really wanted war, the dye for the eruption of a series of new Yugoslav wars was cast between Tudjman and Milošević. The violent secession of Slovenia and Croatia, introducing the harsh and atrocious treatment of the civilian population by all combatants, proved to be only the beginning.

3. Setting the Context

Presently, as this study was going to press in the Fall of 1995, with intense fratricidal war already raging throughout the former Yugoslavia for more than four years, the Balkans are on the verge of an explosion that, if not prevented in time, could rock the whole of Europe, bring war to the entire continent, and disrupt world order. It is virtually inevitable that the US will then be drawn into yet another European-turned-World War.

The tragedy of the situation in the former Yugoslavia is that both the current and anticipated escalations could have been avoided had the West, led by the US, examined the relevant facts and closely studied the situation, rather than commit itself hastily to a policy based on intentional disinformation and sentimentalism generated by largely distorted TV images.

The internal strife in the Balkans, and not just the former Yugoslavia, is of historic ramifications and intensity. Neither "Western logic", nor international outrage and intervention, are capable of suppressing this long-overdue historical cataclysm, let alone preventing its completion. However, it *is* possible to expedite the solution of the process while markedly reducing the levels of violence in the former Yugoslavia.

Tragically, the US-led West, is currently preoccupied with the wrong aspect of the crisis in the former Yugoslavia. Therefore, both the good-intentioned and the cynical manipulative efforts to impose a solution only aggravate the situation. Meanwhile, Germany is pushing for an explosion of the Balkans for its own self-interest. Russia, mesmerized by the rediscovery and legitimization of its Slavonic past and future, is out to settle historic scores. Obsessed with its own traumatic clash with the Westernized world order, the Muslim World uses the Balkan crisis as a spark for a new, self-cleansing *jihad* against Judeo-Christian values and civilization.

The Yugoslav crisis is essentially a quest for national self-determination as well as for a just solution for historic injustices and grievances. However, it is being rapidly transformed into both a religious war and a global crisis: both constituting a potential catalyst and prelude to a new world war. Hence, unless the Balkan crisis is defused immediately, and in a manner that genuinely stabilizes internal dynamics and rifts, the external interventions will increase the interregional pressure, pushing the Balkans, the rest of Europe, and possibly the rest of the world, over the brink.

4. Changing Europe

The present strategic situation in the former Yugoslavia is starkly reminiscent of the strategic dynamics around the turn of the century. Then, as now, several *blocs* maneuvering in a multi-polar environment were forced into a bi-polar environment only to erupt in violence. Eighty years ago, the primary point of friction was in the Balkans. In 1914, one spark in Bosnia was sufficient to bring about an explosion of the building tensions throughout Europe, and subsequently all over the world. That one incident in Sarajevo, which served as the excuse and catalyst for an explosion now called World War I, which, in its own turn, led to World War II and the Cold War, should not be forgotten or ignored. With social, political and economic tensions rapidly building throughout Europe, the continent is increasingly vulnerable to the cataclysmic impact of yet another single incident in Sarajevo.

The likelihood of such an incident taking place is growing under present conditions and circumstances. Presently, the key protagonists in the Balkans are immersed in last-minute preparations for a marked escalation in the war: a dramatic breakout anticipated as of the Spring of 1995. Indeed, there was a marked escalation in the fighting throughout the former Yugoslavia since the Spring of 1995, and the beginning of the spread of Islamist terrorism into Western Europe indeed happened in

August 1995. The consequent, and still escalating, horrendous war is at the very same time the war which most local powers are desperate to prevent, and the war they are convinced is quite inevitable. It is still possible that the West will be drawn into active participation in this Balkan war. Consequently, the Balkans are once again the focus and catalyst of the traditional European power realignment. The European *blocs* emerging in the wake of the cold war are strikingly similar to those on the eve of World War I.

The present situation is, however, far more dangerous than a century ago. The main reason is the rise, and direct involvement in the Balkans, of two major players from outside the traditional European power equation and dynamics: the United States of America and the Islamic Republic of Iran. By intervening in a pure European dynamic and power polity, these two external players are not only derailing the proper course of the European revival, but are also pushing Europe, and the rest of the world, into a new cataclysmic eruption: perhaps a world war.

In modern times — the last three to four centuries — Europe has been comprised of three power *blocs*:

    1. The Western seafaring nations led by Great Britain and France.
    2. The industrialized center led by Germany.
    3. The Slavic east dominated by Russia.

Until some 50 years ago, these *blocs* were floating in a flexible strategic environment influenced by often contradictory economic and political interests in Europe, as well as strategic and economic interests in the Third World (then mostly colonized by the Europeans).

During the Cold War, these European *blocs* were forced into an artificial and rigid bi-polarization. The first two *blocs* rallied behind the US as a counter to the strategic might of the USSR which, in turn, dominated Russia's traditional domains. This bi-polarization, made necessary by the prevailing conditions of the global nuclear stand-off, nevertheless remained artificial. Indeed, the bi-polarization began to crumble in the mid-1980s once the intensity of the Cold War was reduced, even before the fall of the Berlin Wall. By now, this bi-polarization has already disappeared from the European socio-political scene.

The revival of the three European *blocs* has already had direct impact on global politics and economy.

For several centuries now, the strategic posture and economic development of all European *blocs* has largely been determined by trade with, and influence over, segments of the Third World.

1. Britain and France reach out to Africa, the Middle East and littoral Asia through the eastern Mediterranean: Italy and Greece.

2. Germany concentrates on the non-Arab Muslim northern tier — Turkey, Iran, and Afghanistan, and onward into central and east Asia — through a land drive via the Balkans.

3. Russia historically reaches out along a southwards arc ranging from the Slavic south-west in the Balkans all the way eastwards toward China, arching over the land adjacent to Russia, primarily central and south Asia.

Thus, for all three European *blocs*, the Balkans have always constituted the gateway to their key interests in the Third World, and hence, have had great influence on the ability of the European powers to wage the Great Game in the vast expanses of the Third World. The repeated crises and wars in the Balkans in the last centuries were first and foremost manifestations of the struggles between the European powers for hegemony over the gateway to the Orient.

The Cold War did not diminish these traditional trends; merely froze them for half a century: a brief interlude from an historical point of view. These traditional trends and tensions resurfaced as soon as the inter-European power dynamic was revived. Hence, the current crisis in the former Yugoslavia, although initiated and fueled by an indigenous quest for self-determination by the local nations, cannot be separated from its rôle as a manifestation of the revival of the European traditional geo-strategic dynamics.

Indeed, dramatic twists and turns in the wars in the former

Yugoslavia have been, more than anything else, manifestations of the dramatic shifts in the European power structure during both the last phases of the Cold War bi-polarization and the ensuing surge for the revival of the traditional multi-pole posture. These externally induced factors must be coupled with the lingering legacy of the character of the various branches of the southern Slavs.

5. Local Roots

The two main peoples of the former Yugoslavia — the Croats and the Serbs — have themselves been molded and formed over the years by accumulating historic experiences. It should be stressed that these national experiences have been largely shaped by these nations' respective rôles as the pawns guarding the gateways of Europe in the Balkans.

The dominant factor determining the intensity of the current war is that the two main nations of Yugoslavia developed and were molded under different types of foreign dominance for hundreds of years: virtually their entire modern history. Therefore, by the time both Serbs and Croats merged into independence in the 20th century, each of them had already had a very distinct yet diverse legacy and concept of political culture, economic development, as well as socio-religious consciousness.

Under the Germanic influence, the Croats and Slovenes became Catholic and Westernized. In contrast, the Serbs, Macedonians, and Montenegrins developed under a harsh and hostile Turkish rule which resulted in economic backwardness. Consequently, these nations were molded by the "oriental politics and culture" which still dominates their national behavior, irrespective of their religion: Orthodox Christianity or Sunni Islam.

These dramatically different historical experiences and heritage shape the political culture of the dominant southern Slav nations, particularly in the ways they deal with each other.

The Orthodox Christian Serbs — molded by a series of epic and defiant revolts, as well as stoic resistance to, and suffering under, Turkish repressions — tend to favor centralized authoritarian leadership and believe in decisive military solutions which will ensure lingering tangible results. The Serbs are committed to self-reliance against an inherently hostile world around them.

In contrast, the Croats, closely associated with the Austro-Hungarian Empire, matured under the soft Hungarian and Germanic rule, and learned to achieve gains through political cunning, passive resistance, and socio-economic obstructionism. Consequently, Croats tend to concentrate on appealing to, and exploitation of, foreign contacts and influence.

These inherent differences between the political culture and awareness of Serbs and the Croats still dominate their national consciousness and the character of their present struggle for national liberation and self-determination in the new Balkans.

It is impossible to comprehend the current power structure and savage fratricidal wars in the former Yugoslavia without addressing the legacy of World War II. This is an issue which affects everyday life and consciousness and not because of the lingering effect of the pervasive education and indoctrination of the communist era. In the most affected areas, all of them predominantly Serb-populated, the suffering and carnage were so immense that, 50 years after the end of the war, the demographic balance and distribution of the local population is yet to return to the pre-war trends. With two whole generations growing up in families missing relatives due to wartime atrocities and killing, it is impossible for today's youth to disengage from the legacy of the war.

The German and Italian armies invaded Yugoslavia on April 6, 1941. Organized resistance collapsed after two weeks of fierce fighting. Soon afterwards, Yugoslavia was dismembered, some of its borderlands annexed by the participating Axis powers. The bulk of the Yugoslavian territory was divided between a German occupation zone which was predominantly Serbian populated, and the Independent State of Croatia which immediately joined the Axis Powers, contributing considerable forces and assets to the war effort in the Balkans and especially to the German Eastern Front.

Immediately after the German-Italian invasion, Ante Pavelic, the leader of the *Ustaše* movement, established the fascist state of Croatia as a satellite of the Axis powers. In the Summer of 1941, Zagreb declared war on the USSR and sent Croat forces to fight with the Germans on the Eastern front. In December 1941, Croatia also declared war on the US and Britain. In Croatia itself, adopting German occupation policies, the *Ustaše* evolved into an SS-type police force and established a concentration and death camp in Jasenovac, the only non-German death camp in Europe. The *Ustaše* embarked on what they called an "ethnic cleansing" campaign (a phrase coined by the Croatian extremists), rounding up Serbs, Jews and Gypsies. All together at least 500,000 to 700,000 Serbs, Jews and Gypsies (but overwhelmingly Serbs) died in Jasenovac alone in the 1,335 days and nights which the camp operated. It is noteworthy that immediately after he assumed power in 1991, President Tudjman ordered the complete destruction of the Jasenovac camp, which had been preserved and turned into one of Yugoslavia's main war memorials, in order to establish a "rare bird sanctuary" in its place.

During World War II, several Croat and Bosnian Muslim units actively served on the Axis side, mostly under SS command. The Croat forces included 160,000 Domobrani regulars and a 75,000 strong *Ustaše* militia who dealt primarily in "internal security". With a *carte blanche* from the Germans, the Independent State of Croatia unleashed the *Ustaše* on the local Serb population in a campaign of terror aimed at forcing their eviction so that a pure Croatia could be established. In addition, Croat volunteers manned two SS divisions and three *Wehrmacht* divisions, as well as an élite Croat Legion which served under German Command on the Eastern Front. Guided by the former Mufti of Jerusalem, Hajj Amin al-Husseini, the Bosnian Muslim population established several units under the SS command: most notably the 13 SS Handzar Division which had a distinct Muslim character (including public prayer sessions and Qur'anic studies) which was to spearhead Hitler's surge to the Middle East. Ultimately, the Bosnian Muslim units and particularly the Handzar Division joined the *Ustaše* forces in their terror campaigns against the Serbs in areas known today as western Bosnia-Herzegovina and the Krajina.

Meanwhile, two armed resistance movements sprang into action immediately. The communist forces were led by a Croatian activist named Josip Broz, who used the *nom de guerre* Tito. The second was a royalist-nationalist movement led by Col. Draza Mihailović of the Royal Army. Echoing the Soviet propaganda, Tito's movement adopted the name *Partisans* while Mihailović's people were generally known as *ćetniks*, the historical name of Serbian irregular fighters associated with past fighting against the Turks and other foreign invaders.

The guerilla war was waged mainly in Serbian populated areas. Mihailović fought for the interest of the Yugoslav, mainly Serbian, people within the context of the Allied cause. Tito fought for communist power in post-War Yugoslavia within the context of the Soviet-led Great Patriotic War. Although both movements and leaders were fiercely committed to fighting the Axis powers, this dichotomy in their perception of the future of Yugoslavia would dominate their strategies, especially their approach to waging war against the Germans, and ultimately, each other.

Brigadier Sir Fitzroy Maclean, who served as a senior British liaison officer with the Tito Headquarters during World War II, described the difference in approaches to waging the guerilla war in Serbia. At first, both movements conducted a joint struggle against their common enemy. "The rising which took place in Serbia in the Summer of 1941 was essentially a national rising. In it, *Partisan* and *četnik* bands fought side by side. It was astonishingly successful." Consequently, already seeking to divert as many forces as possible to the Eastern Front, the Germans embarked on a fierce suppression of the guerillas and the population. They retaliated for the guerilla attacks by savage reprisals against the civilian population. Maclean stresses that the immensity of these German atrocities brought about the conflict between Mihailović and Tito:

> "In the eyes of the *četniks* the results achieved by their operations could not justify the damage and suffering caused to the civilian population. Their aim was to preserve rather than to destroy. ... The *Partisans*, on the other hand, with true communist ruthlessness, refused to let themselves be deterred by any setbacks or any reprisals from accomplishing the tasks which they set for themselves. Their own lives were of no account. As for the civilians, they too were in the firing-line, with the same chance of a hero's death as they themselves. The more civilians the Germans shot, the more villages they burned, the more enemy convoys the *Partisans* ambushed, the more bridges they destroyed."

In the Spring of 1993, Dobrica Ćosić, the Serb communist and onetime *Partisan* leader turned anti-Tito dissident writer, and, ultimately, the President of the new Yugoslavia, reflected on the historic legacy of World War II. Mihailović fought for a romantic notion of a Yugoslavia that would never exist. "The *Četnik* movement was tragic and anachronistic in its ideas and political views. It had a banal slogan that was intended to win over the peasant masses: *For King and Fatherland!*" The ultimate objective of Mihailović, Ćosić stressed, was the salvation of the Serbian population. Therefore, once the slaughter of Serbs reached the level of affecting the demographic character of Yugoslavia, priority had to be given to preserving the people, especially as Germany was already losing the war and Soviet forces were advancing into the Balkans. Ćosić now acknowledged that, in retrospect, it "was irrational to wage war at the price we paid in Serbia".

In a sharp contrast, the communist *Partisans* continued their war irrespective of the horrendous retribution inflicted by the Germans and Croats on the civilian population, completely oblivious to the suffering of the people for whose liberation the partisans insisted they were fighting. "Such a war could have only been waged by fanatics, people who were not only fighting for Serbia but for Russia as well and wanted to defend the whole world against fascism," explained Ćosić, himself a former *Partisan* officer and commissar.

These distinctions were not merely historical reflections. The trauma of World War II still dominates the psyche of the people of Yugoslavia, directly affecting their current determined and vicious armed struggle, including the horrific cruelty toward each other. Significantly, however, the *Partisans* cooperated frequently with the Germans and the *Ustaše* when the opportunities arose to massacre their rivals, the Mihailović nationalists. It was ironic that, in victory assisted by the Soviet Red Army, the *Partisans* succeeded in accusing the nationalists (the *ćetniks*) and Mihailović in particular, of having aided and abetted the Germans.

The fact is that during World War II, all the Balkan communities, and fragments thereof, engaged in a savage civil war characterized by mutual atrocities which could not be erased by the rise of a post-War Yugoslavia. The subsequent imposition of integration and nation-building policies was unable to erase the legacies of bloodshed, only to subdue them. Indeed, the integrated institutions and elements to have emerged from the war, most notably the Communist Party of Yugoslavia (CPY)-led *Partisan* army which evolved from Tito's forces, were the result of prevailing circumstances rather than the free choice of most participants. For example, Serbs in Croatia, subjected to the atrocities of the *Ustaše*, had no alternative but to join Tito's *Partisan* Army, although it was dominated by Croat communists, because it was the sole local alternative to enduring the *Ustaše*. In Serb-dominated areas, the resistance organizations followed the traditions of fighting the Turks, and units were organized accordingly on a local basis. These were Serb-dominated forces, with heavy Montenegrin presence and leadership, which were isolated in the mountains and largely lacked a political component. This fact would remove them from the post-War power structure.

The revival of Croatian nationalism in the 1980s and 1990s

was indistinguishable from the revival of the *Ustaše*: its chequered coat-of-arms and other nazi-era symbols. Zagreb repeatedly stressed the continuity, causing fear among the Serbs. The Croatian militias drove these fears home when they attempted to assert Zagreb's control over parts of the Krajina and Slavonia explicitly evoking the *Ustaše*'s "return" to these areas.

Therefore, when the young *Ustaše*, wearing the same uniforms as their World War II predecessors, waving the same chequered banners, shouting the same Croat militant chauvinistic slogans, returned to Slavonia in such a flagrant and arrogant way in the Summer of 1991, it had a shocking impact. Little wonder that a few elderly Serbs, all of them survivors of the 1942 massacre and the *Partisan* struggle, snapped: a few of them shooting their shotguns and hunting rifles at the *Ustaše*. The *Ustaše* returned the shots with automatic weapon fire, inflicting casualties among the Serbs. Young Serb militiamen, also equipped with automatic weapons, rushed in and intervened in the firing.

A brief though intense clash ensued. There were a few fatalities on both sides. The *Ustaše* withdrew before darkness fell, vowing to return and take revenge. It was then that the Serb population concluded gloomily that the years of Communist Yugoslavia were but an illusion of co-existence, and that the hated and dreaded Croats had not really changed. This grim realization, made in the immediate aftermath of the shock and clash, would determine the rural population's position in the ensuing crisis. It was imperative, the local Serb leaders argued now, to prepare to defend the Serbs against the specter of renewed atrocities.

In the Summer of 1991, there were too many villages, and too many identical clashes, for each to be labeled an isolated incident. There was, in fact, a concentrated wave of demonstrations of Croatian chauvinism in the heart of one of the Serb areas most affected by Croat atrocities during World War II. Zagreb only increased the significance of this wave of incidents. When the news of these clashes spread, Tudjman and official

Zagreb failed to demonstrate sympathy and understanding to the Serb population of Croatia. Nor did they condemn these attacks, let alone take steps against the young *Ustaše* perpetrators.

The Serbs, with good reason, concluded that these incidents were the beginning of an intentional campaign to evict them from the lands of their ancestors. It would be, they reasoned, a campaign identical to the *Ustaše's* murderous campaigns during World War II.

The fears of the Serbs were not calmed down by the publication of maps of Greater Croatia — the so-called Historical Croatia — which included large segments of Bosnia and parts of Serbia. These maps also included a portrait of Ante Pavelic, the wartime leader of Croatia and the *Ustaše*, and the ideologue of the slaughter committed against Serbs and Jews.

The Sarajevo leadership was also quick to assert its legitimacy by invoking ghosts from World War II. But in mid-1993, Sarajevo revived the Handzar Division with all its fascist culture and preoccupation with the division's rôle as the worthy successor to its SS predecessors. The Bosnia-Herzegovina Handzar Division provides the praetorian guards for Izetbegović and other senior leaders of Sarajevo, clearly reflecting their pride in and support for the revival of the old traditions.

The Bosnian Serbs, descendants of victims of the original Handzar Division and/or the *Ustaše*, could not but fear the greater ramifications of this trend. This time, however, the younger generation of Serbs was determined to ensure that the slaughter and atrocities against their people would not be repeated, whatever the price. It was this sentiment which dominated the Serbian approach to waging their war against the Croats and the Bosnian Muslims in the early 1990s. The first skirmishes and clashes in the various Serb villages in Croatia would prove, in the long run, to have been of crucial importance to the further deterioration of the situation in the Balkans and the eruption of the vicious war. The Serbs, Croats and Bosnian Muslims revived their vicious fighting of World War II, thus determining the totality, cruelty and intensity of the fighting throughout the former Yugoslavia.

In retrospect, the distinct national character of the two dominant protagonists in the former Yugoslavia, strongly reinforced by the trials and legacy of World War II, was too close to the Cold War's divide line not to affect the initial European approach to the break-up of Yugoslavia in the early 1990s.

At first, the Europeans took sides in the intra-Yugoslavian crisis as part of the retention of the Cold War's bi-polarity. Thus, the UK and France followed Germany to support the "Westernized" Croats and Slovenes against the "Slavic" or "Eastern" Serbs commonly associated with the USSR-turned-Russia, then still considered inherently hostile to the West.

Although brief and militarily small, the secession of Croatia and Slovenia was a major event effecting the transformation of the key players. The war started with a Yugoslav Government in Belgrade — including numerous non-Serbs, mostly Croats, at the top — ordering the national army to defend the unity and territorial integrity of the Yugoslav state against unilateral secession. This was well within the framework of the Helsinki Accords which held existing national borders to be inviolable.

However, the ensuing clash evolved into a more compounded phenomenon. The war in Slovenia was an effort by the local Slovenian Territorials to surround and suffocate the local JNA garrisons and ambush and negate JNA attempts to move convoys to relieve the besieged installations. The local paramilitary forces exploited fully the JNA's orders and reluctance to fire on civilians, even if hostile, in order to repeatedly ambush convoys in inhabited areas. Consequently, the JNA was rapidly demoralized, its military effectiveness plummeted.

The war in Croatia was even more demanding from a non-military point of view. In Croatia, as described above, the chauvinistic demons of World War II came out of the closet. For the Croats, the essence of the war was more than gaining independence from Yugoslavia. Their objective was the establishment of a Croat State: that is, evicting the Serb population or, at the very least, discriminating against them thus forcing them to leave "voluntarily".

Consequently, the war in Croatia developed into a series of assaults on inhabited areas — from isolated villages to cities — with the declared aim to determine through the use of force the ethno-demographic character of the area. Croat regular and irregular forces attacked Serb civilians, intentionally committing atrocities aimed at forcing the community to flee. The Serb irregular and JNA organized forces reacted with a vengeance, committing equally horrific atrocities in the process against the local Croats. Some of the fiercest fighting which followed in and around urban centers in eastern Slavonia was exceptionally cruel.

Taken together, the fighting in Slovenia, and particularly Croatia, changed the entire former Yugoslavia irreversibly. Most important has been the transformation of the JNA. The JNA entered the war as a multi-ethnic conscript army. The JNA was the country's most truly integrated institution with a professional cadre committed to the unity of Yugoslavia. By early 1992, it was a completely different institution. The cumulative impact of mass desertion of Croats and Slovenes, the ugly confrontation with the Croat and Slovene hatred, and the deployment to protect Serb villages in Krajina and Slavonia against Croat atrocities: all, when taken together, brought about the Serbianization of the JNA. The JNA's manpower was now predominantly Serb (although there were numerous Bosnian Muslims in senior positions in the JNA during the fighting in eastern Slavonia, presently an enduring source of contention between the Bosnian Muslim forces and their Croat counterparts). Its missions were increasingly to defend Serb civilians against Croat forces. As the JNA was compelled to vacate its garrisons and withdraw into the new Yugoslavia (Serbia and Montenegro), it was becoming increasingly nationalist Serb.

In the Winter of 1991-92, Zagreb sought to suppress some of the key positions held by the Krajina Serbs, especially their hold over key bridges overlooking the Adriatic coast. The Croats also sought to contain the JNA and Slavonian Serb pressure on key cities such as Osijek. The key to Zagreb's strategy was preventing, or at the very least limiting, Belgrade's ability to dispatch reinforcements to bolster the local Serb forces. The main instrument of the Croats was to deploy forces into Croat populated areas in Bosnia-Herzegovina, and subsequently to incite the local Muslim population to join the war against the Serbs.

Zagreb enticed Sarajevo to cross the line and take sides by promising Western diplomatic recognition and massive economic aide. Consequently, the Croats manipulated the situation in the former Yugoslavia to have the Bosnian Muslims become their instrument and point of clash with the Serbs (meaning, doing the killing and dying for the Croats). Zagreb and Bonn then dragged the Western powers into recognizing, and then siding with, the Bosnian Muslims as a legitimate political entity in the Balkans. By now, however, the Bosnian Serbs were resolved to defend their own traditional habitation areas against the resurrection of anti-Serb chauvinism and militancy. With that, the center of the war moved to Bosnia-Herzegovina. Meanwhile, the first cycle of fighting in Croatia ended in the Spring of 1992 with UN forces assuming protection of the local Serb population as JNA forces withdrew from Croatia and Slovenia.

The end of the first phase of the wars in the former Yugoslavia in the Spring of 1992 was much more than moving the center of gravity into Bosnia-Herzegovina (where it remained with the exception of the 1995 Croat onslaught on the Krajina Serbs). With this shift of the fighting, there effectively ended the legacy Cold War constraints on the position and posture of the various European powers. Indeed, it did not take long for Europe, now freed from the artificial bi-polarizing pressure of the Cold War, to return to the traditional and historic three-*bloc* dynamics and fluid alignment. There has since been a corresponding change in the European powers' expectations from their proxies in the Balkans. This has already led to a change in the nature of

European support for the belligerents in the former Yugoslavia.

By the mid 1990s, Europe has fully returned to formulating its policy according to the traditional "normal *blocs*". The most dominant trend is the resurrection of a Russo-German co-existence against the Western sea-faring nations. Russia and Germany are engaged in a condominium-type relationship in order to exploit eastern Europe, as well as conduct a joint surge into, and hegemony over, the Orient (Turkey, Iran, and Central Asia).

In the Balkans, their common gateway to the Orient, the vested interest of both Russia and Germany is now to contain the violence so that they can concentrate on their larger and more important global aspirations. Both Moscow and Bonn therefore now support the establishment of a tenuous co-existence between Croats and Serbs largely along the original Karadjordjevo Agreement of March 1991 on the division of Bosnia-Herzegovina, and the consequent establishment of unified Croatia and Serbia. Despite the periodic flare-up of heavy fighting between Serbs and Croats, both Belgrade and Zagreb have repeatedly reaffirmed the validity of these principles as the basis for the preferable long-term solution for the former Yugoslavia.

The largely-unknown Karadjordjevo Agreement is the result of a series of bilateral meetings held between Tudjman and Milošević in Karadjordjevo, Vojvodina, in early March 1991. In a rare moment of clairvoyance and responsibility, the two leaders seriously examined the long-term aspirations and interests of their nations and sought ways to reconcile between them. Both leaders realized and agreed that what was then happening in Yugoslavia was a resurgence of a popular quest for national self-determination. There was no doubt that the two main nations of the western Balkans — Serbs and Croats — were determined to reunify their peoples, irrespective of the remnants of the Titoist borders, and realize their quest for self-determination.

Milošević and Tudjman concluded that the only way to curb the violence in Yugoslavia was to expedite the process of establishing a new Croatia and a new Serbia, encompassing the majority of Croats and Serbs, each under a single government respectively. The main issue was the Serb and Croat population in Bosnia-Herzegovina, which both leaders considered an artificial entity created by Tito to suppress their own peoples. In Karadjordjevo, Tudjman and Milošević reached a detailed and specific agreement on the carving up of Bosnia-Herzegovina, between their countries. Croatia was to get Herzegovina and Posavina in the north, covering a large portion of World War II Croatia. Milošević secured control over the predominantly-Serb areas. The original agreement called for Serbia to get 75 percent of Bosnia-Herzegovina, and Croatia 25 percent.

A year later, confronted with the West's determination to secure a Muslim state in Bosnia-Herzegovina, Zagreb and Belgrade re-examined their 1991 agreement. They decided that if there would be no escape from retaining a Muslim mini-state: the Serbs would keep only 65 percent of Bosnia-Herzegovina, the Croats would get only 20 percent, leaving the Muslims with 15 percent of the territory. As late as the Autumn of 1994, both Zagreb and Belgrade reiterated their commitment to, preferably, the original Karadjordjevo Agreement, and, if inevitable, the 1992 readjustment of the maps. In the February 1992 meeting in Lisbon, the leaders of the three main groups in Bosnia-Herzegovina, including Izetbegović, agreed on a modified version of the original agreement between Belgrade and Zagreb which would transform Bosnia-Herzegovina into a canton-style state in which all nations could preserve their self-identity. However, at the last moment, Izetbegović reversed himself on the basis of US enticements and promises of support. Later that Spring, the building internal tensions throughout Bosnia resulted in the outbreak of the still ongoing fratricidal war.

Meanwhile, the rise of the Sarajevo regime has proven a major factor in bringing the Western seafaring nations to support the Russo-German solution for the Balkans even though such a posture would reduce their own influence over the former Yugoslavia. The reason for such a dramatic change is the widespread recognition of the threat inherent in the spread of radical Islam into Europe. Thus, the entire Europe — all three *blocs* — is presently determined to speedily contain the spread of militant Islam, including the blocking of its European springboard: Izetbegović's Bosnia-Herzegovina. Europe has already resigned itself to accepting the conclusion that the only viable solution for the crisis in the former Yugoslavia is to enable both Croats and Serbs to realize their burning desire for national self-determination: the establishment of cohesive Serbia and Croatia with their natural boundaries. In the Fall of 1995, the European powers have finally accepted this reality and are already working to implement it.

6. Sarajevo's Way

By now, however, the situation in Bosnia-Herzegovina has already become far too complicated to simply be defused through recognition of reality and implementation of the long sought-after indigenous solutions. This grim reality is the direct outcome of the evolution and transformation of the wars in Bosnia-Herzegovina. Although the Serbs and Croats constitute a majority of the population of Bosnia-Herzegovina, the evolution of the war was dominated by the Bosnian Muslims and the out-of-region powers intervening ostensibly on their behalf.

The convoluted, and extremely cruel war in Bosnia-Herzegovina has transformed since the early 1990s from fratricidal struggles for national self-determination by the local peoples/nationalities into a still-contained war by proxies in which such alien and out-of-region powers as the US and Iran as well as the various European *blocs* (both together and separately) fight for the balance of power in, and the shape of, a future Europe. Both the European and the out-of-region powers struggle for their long-term interests on the backs of the southern Slavs, irrespective of religion and definition of nationality.

The struggle for the future of Bosnia-Herzegovina is the focal point where the future of the entire Balkans, and perhaps the rest of Europe and even the West as a whole, will be decided. It is therefore of great importance to understand the dynamics of the evolution of the war in Bosnia-Herzegovina.

If one follows the Western media (beyond the specter of atrocities and other humanitarian issues), the war in Bosnia-Herzegovina *appears* as a series of unrelated localized clashes, each of which attracts and dominates international attention and involvement for a while. However, in retrospect and from a strategic point of view, one can see that the war in Bosnia-Herzegovina has been evolving according to a very coherent course, while the actual military operations can be divided into three phases in each of which the implementation of the over-riding war aims has been improved. From the very beginning, the course of the war has been dominated by Sarajevo, even when the Bosnian Muslim forces were militarily virtually irrelevant and the Bosnian Serb forces were vastly superior to all. Sarajevo's dominance over the evolution of the war in Bosnia-Herzegovina is the result of the work of Alija Ali Izetbegović and Rasim Delić.

All this time, the Bosnian Serbs have remained committed to preserving their gains; a passive strategic approach leaving the initiative to their opponents. On the eve of the war, Bosnian Serbs had legal title to more than 60 percent of the territory of Bosnia-Herzegovina. The bulk of their initial military operations was to improve their defensive positions and lines of communications, both internally and with Serbia. Once these missions were completed, the Bosnian Serb forces tried to remain on the defensive. In principle, observed General Charles G. Boyd (until the Summer of 1995 the Deputy Commander in Chief, US European Command), "the [Bosnian] Serbs are not trying to conquer new territory, but merely to hold on to what was already theirs". In retrospect, Pale's greatest strategic-political failure to date is this relinquishing of the strategic initiative at the time.

As early as 1992, Izetbegović outlined a very precise and uncompromising strategic political objective for the Sarajevo regime: to get the West to defeat the Serbs and establish a Muslim-dominated state for him. There was no ambiguity about Izetbegović's objectives. Canadian Army Maj.-Gen. Lewis Mackenzie in the Summer of 1992 (when he was UNPROFOR's commander) described the essence of Sarajevo's strategy: "Izetbegović wants the entire country back. Quite frankly, the only way he can get it is by convincing the international community to intervene with massive military force, ridding him of his Serbian enemies. ... It's in the interest of Izetbegović to keep the fighting going, in the hope that the world will come to his rescue — provided he can make it look as if the Serbs are solely responsible for perpetrating the chaos."

The task of both building the Bosnian Muslim armed forces and using them to provoke and instigate that international, essentially Western, military intervention was entrusted to Rasim Delić, the commander of the Muslim Bosnia-Herzegovina Army. Back in 1992, Delić, in his formal capacity as the head of Department for Strategic Planning and the then *de facto* commander of the Muslim forces in Bosnia-Herzegovina, devised a long-term plan which still dominates Sarajevo's military activities. (In the late 1980s, Delić used to be the Chief of the Department of Strategic and Operational Planning of the Yugoslav General Staff.) Delić's plan defined a long-term military build-up and warfare strategy to meet both the need to instigate Western intervention and then enable the Muslim forces to conduct a major war against both Serbs and Croats on their own. This plan is still being implemented quite successfully despite its cynical and manipulative character, as well as Sarajevo's overall Islamist and thus inherently anti-West character. Indeed, the overall course of the wars in Bosnia-Herzegovina since 1992 fit the key phases of Delić's plan:

Phase One: from the Spring of 1992 until early 1993. This phase was dominated by Sarajevo's struggle for international legitimacy. The Bosnian Muslim leadership in Sarajevo was determined not only to ensure that the Western recognition of Bosnia-Herzegovina as a state endured, but also to ensure that the West deligitimized the Serb and Croat posturing for the establishment of coherent and cohesive entities — the Republic of Srpska and Herzeg-Bosna respectively. Sarajevo was determined to gain international legitimacy for a unified Bosnia-Herzegovina as a Muslim state to the point that the West would intervene militarily to impose a Muslim-dominated state on the Christian majority (some 70 percent) in Bosnia-Herzegovina.

Sarajevo's main instrument in this phase was the demonization of the Serbs through a media and disinformation offensive in the West (highlighting Serb "atrocities" and "ethnic cleansing"), as well as pin-prick military actions and self-inflicted terrorism (that is, terrorism inflicted on its own people by its own forces, but blamed on the Bosnian Serbs).

Starting in the Summer of 1992, there was a marked escalation in the provocations performed by the Muslim forces in order to instigate a major military intervention by the West against the Serbs and, to a lesser extent, the Croats. Initially, these provocations were mainly senseless attacks on their own Muslim population, but they soon expanded to include attacks on Western and UN objectives.

A UN investigation concluded that several key events which galvanized public opinion and governments in the West to take bolder action in Bosnia-Herzegovina, were in fact "staged" for the Western media by the Bosnian Muslims themselves in order to dramatize Sarajevo's plight. Investigations by the UN and other military experts count among these self-inflicted actions the "bombing" of the bread line (May 27, 1992), the "shelling" of Douglas Hurd's visit (July 17, 1992), the explosion in the cemetery (August 4, 1992), the killing of US broadcaster ABC's producer David Kaplan (August 13, 1992), and the shooting down of an Italian Air Force G.222 transport aircraft on approach to Sarajevo (September 3, 1992). In all these cases Serbian forces were out of range, and the weapons actually used against the victims were not those claimed by the Bosnian Muslim authorities and the parroting Western media.

Ironically, despite evidence of the Izetbegović administration's responsibility for the killing of one of its senior staff, the US ABC network continued to support the Sarajevo leadership and to demonize the Serbs.

The UN concluded that a special group of Bosnian Muslim forces, many of whom had served with Islamist terrorist organizations, committed a series of atrocities, including "some of the worst recent killings", against Bosnian Muslim civilians in Sarajevo "as a propaganda ploy to win world sympathy and military intervention". These attacks escalated into premeditated attacks and atrocities committed against Bosnian Serb civilians trying to flee contested areas. In early September 1992, UN security officials in Geneva pointed out that the shooting down of the Italian transport "was in line with a growing number of Muslim actions intended to scuttle moves toward peace and to provoke outside military intervention". They added that "the Muslims have targeted United Nations troops and even other Muslims in the capital of Bosnia to throw blame on the Serbs".

Ultimately, through cynical manipulation of a susceptible Western media and a lavishly financed public relations blitz, the Bosnian Muslims and their then Croat allies were indeed able to demonize the Serbs and twist the image of the fighting in Bosnia-Herzegovina to such an extent that this twisted perception of Bosnia-Herzegovina still prevails and dominates the decisionmaking of the Clinton Administration in Washington as well as public opinion and populist policies elsewhere in the West.

For their part, the Bosnian Serbs have been inadvertently helping this propaganda blitz aimed at the demonization of the Serbs. In retrospect, Pale's greatest strategic-military mistake was the beginning of the massive shelling of Sarajevo in the Spring of 1992, and subsequently escalating this campaign into laying siege on Sarajevo. Consequently, and unintentionally, Pale has been providing means and opportunity for the Western politicians and their press to transform the complicated Bosnia-Herzegovina issue into the simplistic and emotional presentation of the plight of innocent civilians in Sarajevo. The Bosnian Muslim self-inflicted acts of terrorism, widely attributed to the Serbs, only served to exacerbate the West's preoccupation with the plight of Sarajevo as the essence of the situation in Bosnia-Herzegovina. This development compounded the effects of Pale's strategic-political error in losing the strategic initiative in the region.

Phase Two: from the Spring of 1993 until early 1994. This phase was dominated by the building-up of the Bosnian Muslim Armed Forces in preparation for future offensives, while, at the very same time, strengthening the West's, particularly Washington's, sympathy and commitment to the Bosnian Muslim cause to the point of considering massive military intervention on their behalf. (The unique rôle played by the US is discussed in detail below.) In the Spring of 1993, Sefer Halilović, then commander-in-chief of the Bosnian [Muslim] Army, acknowledged that the Bosnia-Herzegovina forces were "incapable, without outside help, of getting back significant parts of its lost territory".

The Bosnian Muslim military build-up was based on Delić's plan and intended not only to acquire weapons but to transform the Muslim forces (now including numerous foreign volunteers in key positions) and national infrastructure into an offensive-oriented military establishment. During *Phase Two*, Sarajevo was actively preparing for a major escalation in the fighting, first through offensive irregular warfare and, ultimately, regular campaigns, following the arrival of major reinforcements from around the Muslim World.

The most important facet of the strategic build-up was the establishment of well-defended sanctuaries into which reinforcements and weapons shipments could arrive, and from where offensives would ultimately be launched against the Serbs and the Croats. The key sanctuaries were established around air bases protected by medium and long range air defense systems, themselves smuggled into Bosnia-Herzegovina. The main sanctuaries selected are the Dubrave military airbase and heliport near Tuzla, and the Butmir airport near Sarajevo. A wide variety of sophisticated weapon systems, from advanced missiles to heavy artillery pieces, as well as crews and ammunition, were promised by Syria, Turkey, Iran, Egypt, and Saudi Arabia. All can be delivered by C-130-type transport aircraft into the airstrips in the sanctuaries.

Once these sanctuaries were operating and key weapon systems delivered, Delić's plan called for the beginning of offensive military operations on a localized basis. These would be a combination of limited offensives and a spate of irregular warfare, that is terrorism, throughout the Serb and Croat "strategic rear", namely, Croatia and Yugoslavia proper. The local offensives would be carried out by numerous brigade-size, each 6,000-troops strong, élite forces supported by long-range weapons, a growing number of heavy artillery and tanks, as well as helicopter gun-ships and assault helicopters.

Indeed, a major reorganization of the Bosnian Muslim forces into a professional conventional military system has already been completed. In April 1994, Sarajevo established a professional high command, and the army was reorganized into seven corps, each comprised of one to three brigades and regiments, as well as several special forces/*Mujahedin* units. In early 1995, with the beginning of the new cycle of offensives, the Bosnian Muslim forces in the key sectors in central Bosnia were further organized into division-level groupings, each comprised of three or four brigades. This reorganization reflects availability of heavier weapons and standardization of military equipment. Further more, there has been a marked increase in the number and quality of the special forces/*Mujahedin* units which now spearhead all key offensives. In mid-May 1995, the *Mujahedin* forces were organized as the 3rd Corps.

There has been a corresponding increase in the size and arsenal of the Bosnian Muslim forces. By 1994, the overall number of Bosnian Muslim troops reached between 150,000 and 200,000 depending on the extent of mobilization. Their weapons improved markedly, both in quality and in the emergence of an ordinary and lavishly-provided logistical system. Numerous volunteers from Muslim countries were instrumental in transforming the Bosnian Muslim forces into not only a professional army (a feat where the experience and expertise of many Muslim JNA veterans was instrumental) but also impart the zeal of revolutionary militant Islam on an originally secular manpower pool. There were also noticeable improvements in the army's equipment. The small arms and medium size weapons were standardized, and a flow of ammunition secured. The Bosnian Muslims also began to introduce into combat heavy artillery and even tanks from concealed and recently-acquired stockpiles.

The Croatian Armed Forces, meanwhile, virtually absorbed the Bosnian Croat forces (HVO) into their ranks. The "militarized" HVO is about 50,000 strong, and is comprised of six to eight brigades equipped with 130 tanks, 150 artillery pieces, and an assortment of helicopters and light transports. However, the key to the Croat military capabilities in Herzeg-Bosna is the Croatian expeditionary force (ie: from the Republic of Croatia) which size varies on the basis of the conditions in the theater. At its peak, it was 10 to 12 brigades strong (on top of the HVO's). The Croat Armed Forces are constantly improving, absorbing most modern heavy weapons (including tanks, artillery, and missiles) from both East and West. In 1995, some of the best equipped units were deployed to western Bosnia-Herzegovina as part of the assault on Krajina and in preparations for a major offensive into central Bosnia.

In contrast, there is an ongoing degradation in the Bosnian Serb military capabilities. The main reason is the continued attrition of its manpower to battlefield casualties and migration. Between 1993 and early 1995, the Bosnian Serb forces shrunk from about 110,000 troops to 80,000. Deficiencies in maintenance and availability of spares continue to reduce the serviceability of the once-vaunted arsenal of some 1,000 artillery pieces, some 500 tanks, and some 300 APCs (data prior to the US-led NATO bombing of September 1995).

Shortages of fuel have worsened by the embargo imposed by Milošević. The NATO bombing of ammunition depots and production facilities further eroded the Bosnian Serb military capabilities. Until early 1995, the Bosnian Serbs conducted their military operations convinced that the JNA would rush to their aid in case of a setback of significance. Milošević's decision not to intervene on behalf of the Krajina Serbs (discussed in detail below) jolted Pale, causing a major reassessment of the Bosnian Serb military potential. However, the Bosnian Serb forces still enjoy the most professional and competent command structure in Bosnia-Herzegovina, and they should prove capable of meeting the challenges of the new posture.

Meanwhile, the overall military activities during *Phase Two* were mainly sporadic clashes between the Bosnian Muslim forces and both Serbs and Croats in order to increase tension both in the region and all over the world, as well as keep the Sarajevo issue alive. Sarajevo's primary objective at this stage was the stalling of the advance of the Croat and Serb forces through the infliction of unacceptable losses. Toward this end, the Bosnian Muslims acquired large quantities of modern ATGMs [Anti-Tank Guided Missiles], some long range tube artillery and MBRLs [Multiple-Barrel Rocket Launchers]. These weapons, served by expert volunteer crews, enabled the Muslim forces to stabilize their lines and even make several localized tactical gains.

In addition, the Bosnian Muslim forces carried out two distinct major operations: one against the Serbs and one against the Croats. These operations were strategic-political in nature and were not intended to deliver tangible military gains. Their primary objective was to serve as test-runs for the forthcoming escalation which still characterizes *Phase Three*. Further more, the main issue tested was the extent of the West's, and especially Washington's, susceptibility to, and cooperation with, Sarajevo's provocations and aggression.

The fighting around Srebrenica in the Spring of 1993 was the first Bosnian Muslim offensive which was used as a provocation aimed at instigating a Serb counter-offensive and siege. Muslim propaganda would then present the Serb reaction as onslaught on and atrocities against civilians, thus justifying international military intervention. For Sarajevo, the Srebrenica gambit failed militarily because Gen. Philippe Morillon, the French UNPROFOR commander, intervened, and while saving the town from a Serbian occupation in a counter-offensive, also insisted on the disarming of the local Bosnian Muslim forces so that they could no longer provoke a Serbian assault.

However, the Srebrenica operation proved a great success from a political point of view because the Western media coverage reported exactly the disinformation themes stressed by Sarajevo. The Western political reaction did not deviate from these themes. This phenomenon convinced Sarajevo that it would indeed be possible to conduct strategic-level provocation and disinformation campaigns in order to instigate massive military intervention from the West, especially the US. Moreover, the Bosnian Muslim military capitalized on the Srebrenica incident to establish Tuzla as a base for the UN, and thus justified the build-up of Bosnian Muslim capabilities there. In retrospect, Srebrenica served as a "test run" for the series of offensives-provocations which the Bosnian Muslims would launch starting the Spring of 1994.

The other "test run" in the Spring and Summer of 1993 was aimed to serve as a deterrence to the Croats not to actively challenge the growing might and Islamist character of the Bosnian forces. Sarajevo was determined to ensure that the Croats gave up on co-existence with the Bosnian Muslims irrespective of the political rhetoric on the federation and other Croat-Muslim political arrangements.

This deterrence was achieved by unleashing the Islamist *Mujahedin* forces on Travnik and Varez. In the Summer of 1993, the now better-organized and re-equipped Bosnian Muslim forces, led by *Mujahedin* forces, launched a series of offensives aimed at tilting the strategic balance of forces in central Bosnia. They stormed the Travnik and Vitez areas, intentionally committing unprecedented atrocities against the Croat civilian population and seized numerous Croats as hostages.

As the slaughter spread, several Croat civilians escaped

across Serb lines where they received food, medical help and transportation across Croat lines. The "Islamic fanatics" (the Islamists) were directly responsible for the "slaughter" of Croats in Travnik, explained Davor Kolenda, a senior HVO official. "That is why we decided to talk to the commanders of the Armed Forces of the Republic of Srpska, and to our satisfaction we successfully came to an agreement on saving our civilians from the invasion of Islamic evil." In the aftermath of slaughter in central Bosnia-Herzegovina, Kolenda stressed, the HVO leadership and all the area's Croats concluded that "there can be no more co-existence with the Muslims". And this notion is exactly what Sarajevo has sought to impress upon the Croats.

Phase Three: as of the Spring of 1994. This phase has been dominated by the Bosnian Muslim launching of a series of localized offensives; primarily provocations launched from UN-designated safe zones against the Serbs. These offensives were not aimed to deliver military achievements, but rather instigate massive military intervention by the West, especially the US, in order to "save" and consolidate the Sarajevo regime throughout Bosnia-Herzegovina.

Taken together, the still unfolding *Phase Three* constitutes a coherent and sophisticated strategic-political offensive, albeit comprised of a series of smaller and discrete military incidents, optimized to compel and convince the US, and the West as a whole, to intervene militarily in Bosnia in order to consolidate Sarajevo's rule over the entire Bosnia-Herzegovina as well as defeat the Serb forces for the Sarajevo regime. In principle, the main military activity during *Phase Three* has been a series of Bosnian Muslim offensives aimed to, and ultimately succeeding in, instigating massive Serb counter-offensives. These Serbian overreactions have in turn been capitalized on by Sarajevo as an excuse and pretext for its urging the West for a marked expansion of its direct military involvement in Bosnia-Herzegovina against the Serbs.

Phase Three started with a self-inflicted major terrorist provocation. On February 5, 1994, a major explosion rocked the Markale — Sarajevo's main market place — causing heavy casualties. What was immediately described as the ubiquitous "Serb mortar shell" was actually a special charge designed and built with help from *HizbAllah* experts and then most likely dropped from a nearby rooftop onto the crowd of shoppers. Video cameras at the ready recorded this expertly-staged spectacle of gore, while dozens of corpses of Bosnian Muslim troops killed in action (exchanged the day before in a "body swap" with the Serbs) were paraded in front of cameras to raise the casualty counts.

This callous self-killing was designed to shock the West, especially sentimental and gullible Washington, in order to raise the level of Western sympathy to the Bosnian Muslims and further demonize the Serbs so that Western governments would be more supportive of Sarajevo's forthcoming aggressive moves, and perhaps even finally intervene militarily. On the eve of *Phase Three*, it was imperative for Sarajevo to make the West/US even more predisposed to escalating their military intervention in Bosnia-Herzegovina: from tacitly assisting in the wholesale violation of the arms embargo on the Bosnian Muslims, to launching NATO air strikes against the Serb forces, to actually deploying major forces and taking over fighting the Serbs from the Bosnian Muslims. Amazingly, Sarajevo's cynical strategy almost succeeded more than once.

A key by-product, ostensibly of an humanitarian nature but actually of great military importance stemming from the Markale self-inflicted terrorism, was the establishment of the safe-areas and exclusion zones. These areas were established by the UN in order to protect Bosnian Muslim civilian population from the Serbs. In reality, these zones became the core of Sarajevo's offensive military system. The Bosnian Muslims periodically moved forces from one safe area to another in order to concentrate forces for offensives, using the UN and NATO, their troops and airpower, as protectors of the other safe areas; all in the name of humanitarian considerations.

The key military activities during *Phase Three* are the fierce fighting around Muslim cities in Bosnia-Herzegovina starting with the Gorazde crisis in the Spring of 1994. Each of these crises started as a surprise offensive launched by the Bosnian Muslim armed forces from a sanctuary: UN designated safe zones established in early 1994 to protect Muslim civilians. As a rule, when the Bosnian Serb forces blocked the offensive, counter-attacked and pushed the Muslim forces back, Sarajevo's propaganda machine transformed the event from a military confrontation to an international humanitarian crisis. The Western media instigated international outcry over Serb attacks on indefensible refugees in internationally protected sanctuaries, urging the UN/US to use force against the Bosnian Serbs (which manifested itself in pin-prick NATO bombings). That the Bosnian Serb forces tended to over-react and use massive firepower to contain and destroy the numerically superior Bosnian Muslim infantry forces did not help Pale's case and image.

However, the fact remains that in launching these offensives, Sarajevo grossly violated the conditions governing the UN-designated safe zone; conditions clearly and explicitly spelled in legal agreements which Sarajevo had signed.

In the Spring of 1994, in the aftermath of Gorazde, Dutch Brig.-Gen. G.J.M. Bastiaans, the Head of the UN Military Observers (UNMO) in the former Yugoslavia, stressed this issue. "It was the Muslims who provoked the Serbian attack on Gorazde. The Serbs perhaps reacted excessively. But ultimately it was the Muslims who pushed the Bosnian Serb Army to the bloodbath of the civilian population of Gorazde with continual provocations." Brig.-Gen. Bastiaans attributed the Western reaction to a "propaganda campaign" waged by Sarajevo and the West's willfulness to follow cue. "Everyone, including NATO, had walked into it with open eyes," he stressed. "The Muslims provoked the Serbs with shootings and harassment to such a point that they had little option other than using the heavy weapons." US/UN/NATO hypocrisy was extreme throughout the Gorazde crisis. The Bosnian Muslims' mere use of force in Gorazde was never questioned, let alone criticized. However, "officially, the Muslims in the safe areas must surrender their weapons," Brig.-Gen. Bastiaans noted.

The West continued to ignore the realities in Bosnia-Herzegovina, and concentrated instead on the "humanitarian" aspect of the escalating war as depicted by Sarajevo and the Sarajevo-based media. Although the West resisted a massive military intervention, the symbolic actions spoke volumes. Whenever possible, NATO air strikes and other UN activities were designed to demonstrate (even if symbolically) explicit international support for the Bosnian Muslims. The recently-established (1995) UN Rapid Reaction Force is specifically aimed against the Bosnian Serbs. Little wonder, therefore, that Sarajevo has since launched a series of such offensives since the Spring of 1994. The main attacks against the Serbs were at Gorazde, Bihac, Sarajevo, Tuzla (of a lesser magnitude) and most recently Srebrenica, and main attacks against the Croats were at Mostar and Vitez.

It is clear that from a pure military point of view, the Bosnian Muslim forces had little or no chance to defeat the Bosnian Serb forces in any of these offensives. The Muslim forces could, and did, inflict heavy casualties on the increasingly exhausted Bosnian Serb forces. But the impact of these losses on Pale has been a far cry from being able to decide the fate of the war. Sarajevo's High Command, comprised of highly professional officers such as Delić, could not have had such unrealistic and false expectations. Indeed, the primary objective of these offensives was not the Serb forces: it was the Clinton Administration in Washington DC. By subjecting its civilian population to the inevitable Serb excessive use of firepower during their counter-offensives, Sarajevo sought to build international pressure which would ultimately lead to a massive Western military intervention which is what would finally defeat the Serbs.

Although the West did not intervene militarily in a massive manner other than the air campaign launched in late August 1995, all other developments in Bosnia-Herzegovina during

Phase Three clearly confirmed the correctness of Sarajevo's cynical strategy. The military activities of both UNPROFOR and NATO have become distinctly pro-Muslim; US/NATO now formally acknowledged their tacit support for the outright violation of the embargo on Bosnia-Herzegovina, and, more recently, the US began to directly supply the Bosnian Muslim forces with weapons.

The US and the UN tolerated the mounting flow of weapons from Iran and other Muslim states into Croatia during 1994. Due to the intentionally vague definition of the federative arrangements, these weapons found their way to the Bosnian Muslim forces. As of February 1995, on the eve of the first major Muslim surge in Tuzla, there began an intensive and direct supply by air. UN officials complained formally in late February that earlier that month there were several flights of unidentified Lockheed Martin C-130 *Hercules* military transports into the Tuzla area. Nevertheless, the frequency of such flights continued to grow to the point that on June 30, a senior French military officer formally accused the US of supplying weapons, combat intelligence, as well as military expertise to the Bosnian Muslim forces in violation of the embargo. US officials privately acknowledged to European counterparts that the C-130s were from Turkey and other Muslim states but were not US.

That the West ignored the Bosnian Muslim sniper killing of French troops in Sarajevo, and the killing of a Dutch soldier in Srebrenica, only to point a finger at the Bosnian Serbs could not have but confirmed Sarajevo's cynical view of the West. Indeed, instead of ultimately containing the crisis and violence, the war in Bosnia-Herzegovina seems to be escalating out of control. Because the essence of Sarajevo's strategy has remained to instigate a massive foreign military intervention against the Serbs, the level and audacity of the Bosnian Muslim provocations continue to escalate. Consequently, the current Bosnian crisis is far more dangerous because greater dynamics increasingly shape events in the Balkans.

7. The Outsiders

The specter of a global eruption as a result of fighting in the Balkans is increasingly dangerous because of the rise, and direct involvement in the Balkans, of two major players from outside the traditional European power equation and dynamics: the United States of America and the Islamic Republic of Iran. By their mere intervention in a pure European dynamic, these two external players are badly complicating the Balkan crisis, and especially the situation in Bosnia-Herzegovina. This, consequently, is pushing Europe, and the rest of the world, into a new cataclysmic eruption, perhaps a world war.

The United States is acting like a very young, naïve giant, still incapable of coping with a post-Cold War world driven by history, religion and ethno-nationalism. Washington is zigzagging between emotional gut-reaction to manipulations by the visual media, and desperate effort to dominate the new-old world despite Washington's inability to realize, let alone reverse, the changes in the global power structure. Ultimately, the shallowness of the current Clinton Administration makes it vulnerable to the great provocations of the most virulently anti-US players in the Balkan power-play.

It is so befitting Washington's shallowness and culpability, that the Clinton Administration's Balkans policy is based on, and aimed to please, the establishment media. For its part, the

Western visual media — the repeated specter of civilian casualties and sufferings — has become Sarajevo's primary instrument of instigating Western massive military intervention. It is toward this end that the Bosnian Muslims have committed a series of horrendous terrorist strikes against their own people (which the media unfailingly attributed to the Serbs), prevented many of their own citizens from receiving humanitarian aid, and, more recently, launched a series of offensives from UN-designated safe areas in order to compel the West to save them. The Clinton Administration has been eager to act.

To date, the only damper of Washington's eagerness to intervene militarily on the side of the Bosnian Muslims and against the Serbs has been Washington's reluctance to break the NATO consensus with the West Europeans. Meanwhile, Western Europe, which provides the bulk of the troops and officers of UNPROFOR, has belatedly recognized the Bosnian Muslim machinations. Presently, the Europeans — both directly and through NATO and UNPROFOR — are resisting Washington's pressure to be dragged into a wider war by falling into Sarajevo's provocations. "It is not part of our mission to impose any solution through force of arms. We are neither mandated nor deployed for this," Britain's Lt.-Gen. Sir Michael Rose (then the UNPROFOR commander in Sarajevo) stressed in the Autumn of 1994. Across the board, Europe is determined not to deliver a victory for Sarajevo.

While constrained in its daily activities by the Europeans' resolute stand, the Clinton Administration remains determined to ultimately deliver a Bosnian Muslim victory against the demonized Serbs. At the same time, the United States is also striving to reassert its leadership position in Europe by emerging as the peace-maker of the Balkans.

US General Charles G. Boyd, USAF (ret.), deputy Commander-in-Chief, US European Command from November 1992 to July 1995, observed: "[The] US approach to the war in Bosnia is torn by a fundamental contradiction. The United States says that its objective is to end the war through a negotiated settlement, but in reality what it wants is to influence the outcome in favor of the Muslims. ... This duplicity, so crude and obvious to all in Europe, has weakened America's moral authority to provide any kind of effective diplomatic leadership. Worse, because of this, the impact of US action has been to prolong the conflict while bringing it no closer to resolution."

Consequently and bizarrely, it is the United States — the Islamists' "Great Satan" — which has now become the most active and zealous participant in the Islamists' grand design. Completely disregarding the realities in Bosnia-Herzegovina, the US is relentlessly pursuing unilateral policies which not only contradict the declared position of the UN, but, as of the Fall of 1994, have also turned against the US's closest allies in both NATO and Western Europe. The great bafflement is that the Clinton Administration's policy, if continued, will ultimately lead to a European war, perhaps a World War, which serves nobody's interests but that of Iran and the Islamists. They are determined to capitalize on such a war to finally destroy the Great Satan.

Unlike the West, for Iran and the Islamic *bloc* which it is heading, the struggle for and in Bosnia-Herzegovina is but a small phase, albeit of crucial significance, in an historical and global *jihad*: an uncompromising struggle between the West and revivalist Islam. The Islamists — states, organizations and individuals — persistently tailor their specific rôles in Bosnia-Herzegovina to fit the overall long-term strategy. Consequently, by the mid-1990s, the Islamists in Bosnia-Herzegovina have emerged as the western-most segment and eager instrument of the virulently anti-US, Tehran-led Islamic *bloc*. The Islamists consider the mere presence of Western values in the Muslim World a threat to the very existence of Islam. Therefore, since no compromise or even co-existence is possible between the US-led West and Islam, a cataclysmic clash with the US is inevitable. Iran and its allies consider Bosnia-Herzegovina to be their springboard into Western Europe: the next primary theater in this *jihad*.

Sarajevo's Islamist allies have no illusions about the true nature and potential of the current fighting in Bosnia-Herzegovina. Tehran sees two possible outcomes of the crisis in Bosnia-Herzegovina:

The first, and most likely, possibility is that the inevitable suppression of the Bosnian Muslims by the West will serve, according to Tehran's grand design, as the last proof for the vehement anti-Islamic posture of the West. Consequently, the millions of Muslim migrants in Western Europe, and even North America, will take on their "tormentors" — the Western liberal states — and begin the apocalyptic clash between Islam and the West. The massive arrests of Islamist militants conducted in 1995 in France, the UK, and even Germany, clearly demonstrate that the Western powers of Europe are fully aware of the growing threat of militant Islam.

The second, and increasingly remote, possibility is that the Bosnian Muslims will ultimately be able to drag the Western powers, and especially the US, into a fratricidal European war over the Balkans, and ultimately a World War. The Islamists' hope is that in such a World War the West will have attrited and exhausted itself to the extent that it would no longer be able to resist the surge of revolutionary Islam. The Izetbegović regime in Sarajevo is the strongest proponent of this vision. Sarajevo is committed to revive Islam's surge into Europe — last stopped in the 17th Century — by manipulating the Western powers into self-destruction.

These Islamist grand designs are of global strategic importance far exceeding the specter of a future European war. By the mid-1990s, the Islamists have emerged as the western-most segment and eager instrument of the Trans-Asian Axis which is virulently anti-US. In the Balkans, the Tehran-led Islamic *bloc* is spearheading the Beijing-led Trans-Asian Axis. The Iranian and Pakistani intelligence services and military establishments are the most active players inside Bosnia-Herzegovina, despite growing coolness between Tehran and the Pakistani leadership. As a geo-strategic *bloc* of immense economic might in the Pacific Rim, the vested interest of the Trans-Asian Axis is to surge economically. Europe's self-destruction in crisis and war will greatly enhance this chance. This global vision is essentially the modernized phrasing of China's historic vision of the rôle of the Middle Kingdom. In more pragmatic terms, the Chinese, Japanese, and other rising economic powers of the Pacific Rim are determined to slow down and counter-balance the Russo-German surge into the Heart of Asia. An expedient way to prevent a too great a Russo-German embrace is by instigating a crisis in Europe in which the vital interests of Russia and Germany will clash. Hence, the centrality of the struggle in Sarajevo.

8. The Bosnian Jihad

So it is global strategic interests far beyond the immediate European scene which make it imperative for the Islamists — from Tehran's Islamic *bloc* to the Sarajevo leadership — to escalate the war in Bosnia-Herzegovina as well as increasingly give it a distinct Islamist character. Indeed, the primary military modernization and build-up programs in Bosnia-Herzegovina currently underway are Islamist, and the key to foreign reinforcements and weapons supplies is in the Muslim world. Important segments of this build-up take place in the context of world-wide Islamist activities largely associated with international terrorism.

Indeed, the build-up of new Islamist units was completed in Bosnia-Herzegovina in the Spring of 1995. These forces are closely associated with the Armed Islamic Movement (AIM) and Islamist international terrorism, and include the first organized deployment of martyrdom forces (that is, suicide terrorists); both veteran Arabs and newly trained Bosnians. These recent activities were conducted under the guidance of the new Islamist headquarters in Tehran and Karachi, decided upon during the Popular Arab Islamic Conference (PAIC) convened in Khartoum in the first days of April 1995. The Conference decided to establish "new Islamist representative offices" for the international Islamist movement. The new regional center in Tehran will be responsible for Islamist activities (training, equipping, operational support, etc.) in Bosnia-Herzegovina (as well as other politically-sensitive hot spots), while the comparably new center in Karachi would be responsible for Islamist activities in Albania (including Kosovo). Furthermore, this overall Islamist effort and build-up is not just to cope with the situation in the Balkans, but also to be used as a sound base for the Islamists' ability to expand operations into western Europe — mainly France, the UK and Germany — in revenge for any military or diplomatic setback for the Sarajevo administration.

Meanwhile, the leadership of the Armed Islamic Movement (AIM) was formally notified in mid-May 1995 that the "*Mujahedin* Battalion is an officially-recognized army battalion of the Bosnian army; it is comprised of non-Bosnian volunteers, called Ansar, along with Bosnian *Mujahedin*. The formal name of the units is *Armija Republike Bh 3, Korpus Odred el-Mudzahidin*". The commander, an Egyptian "Afghan", was identified as "Ameer Kateebat al-*Mujahedin* Abu al-Ma'ali": a religious-military title and a *nom de guerre*. The Islamist force is based in the Travnik and Zenica areas in central Bosnia.

The AIM senior officials in Sarajevo included in their May 1995 report to the supreme leadership of AIM a strategic analysis of the situation in Bosnia-Herzegovina and the general context of the importance of the *Mujahedin* forces. They wrote that "[the] *Mujahedin* are preparing for major battles, expected to escalate this Summer. Military readiness is at maximum and the Bosnian army is planning to take back its Muslim land from the occupiers." In order to facilitate this escalation, total mobilization was declared in Sarajevo.

The AIM senior officials stressed that Sarajevo was anticipating an all-out war against both the Serbs and the Croats. "Bosnian-Croatian federal unity is becoming more fragile as a result of Croatian actions at the political and military levels. Croatian forces threatened several *Mujahedin* brothers while on their way to *Hajj*, and are continuing their atrocities in the occupied Muslim city of Mostar. There are strong indications that the Croats will back-stab Muslim forces." Despite the seemingly overwhelming odds against the Muslim forces, Sarajevo is confident that the time is ripe for such an escalation.

The AIM report emphasizes that both they — the AIM senior officials in Sarajevo — and the Sarajevo leadership are considering the forthcoming escalatory offensive as "a *jihad* to defend their religion and sacreds (*Hurumat*) against this crazed spiteful crusade". Therefore, they assure their superiors that the Islamists worldwide will do their utmost to support the Bosnian Muslim forces in this endeavor.

The Khartoum, Sudan-based National Islamic Front (NIF) — the political umbrella organization to which AIM answers — did not take long to look for the appropriate solutions for the challenges in Bosnia-Herzegovina. In mid-August 1995, at the height of the US peace drive, the approach of the Islamist leadership in Khartoum and Sarajevo was clarified. NIF examined the situation in Bosnia-Herzegovina in the context of other major theaters of Islamist revolutionary struggle against hostile non-Muslim forces. Khartoum believes that the Muslims of Bosnia share fate and challenge with the Muslims of Kashmir and Palestine, and that the path of *jihad* against their non-Muslim oppressors is essentially identical.

Being a theologically driven movement, the NIF supreme leadership sought legal precedents to serve as a guideline for the nature of *jihad* which they believe should be waged in Bosnia, Palestine, and Kashmir. In mid-August 1995, Khartoum informed the AIM senior officials in the front line — in such places as Sarajevo, Muzzaffarabad (Pakistan), and Damascus — of the precedent found.

The NIF leadership pointed to the text of a *fatwa* originally issued by the Islamic Religious Conference held in El-Obaeid, State of Kordofan (Sudan), on April 27, 1993. It is presently used in Khartoum, at the highest levels of NIF, as the precedent-setting text for legislating relations between Muslims and non-Muslims in areas where the infidels are not willing to be simply subdued by the Muslim forces. The following places — Palestine, Bosnia, and Kashmir — are stated explicitly as areas to where the principles outlined by this *fatwa* are most applicable.

The *fatwa* does not distinguish very much between Muslims seeking co-existence with non-Muslims and secular state authorities, and the non-Muslims resisting the imposition of a Muslim state upon them. "Therefore, the rebels who are Muslims and are fighting against the [Muslim] state are hereby declared apostates from Islam, and the non-Muslims are hereby declared *kaffirs* [infidels] who have been standing up against the efforts of preaching, proselytization, and spreading Islam into Africa. However, Islam has justified the fighting and the killing of both categories without any hesitation whatsoever ..." The April 1993 *fatwa* is a lengthy legal document stipulating in great detail, while citing evidence from the Qur'an, that there is no viable and legal alternative to a most bloody *jihad*. Thus, the NIF leadership is not wrong, from an Islamic legal point of view, in selecting this *fatwa* as a guideline for the Islamist *jihad* strategy in Kashmir, Palestine, and Bosnia.

Meanwhile, Sarajevo's apocalyptic view of the future fits closely with the Islamists' growing anticipation of "gloom and doom" in their relations with the West. Having repeatedly and desperately tried to compel or induce the US-led West to intervene in the Balkan war and endure the brunt of the fighting against the Serbs, Sarajevo is increasingly doubtful about the likelihood of such an eventuality. The Islamist leadership interprets the overall situation in the Balkans as yet more proof of the West's implacable hostility toward Islam, urging Sarajevo to increase its involvement in the avenging Holy War. It is under these conditions that Bosnia's rôle as the European springboard for Islamist terrorism is being consolidated further. The activation of the new *Mujahedin* units are but the very beginning.

The AIM senior officials in Sarajevo reported in mid-May 1995 the completion of "a new camp called Martyrs' Detachment", in order to absorb many newly-arriving *Mujahedin*. These suicide terrorists, including at least a dozen Bosnian

Muslims, graduated from an intensive course in training camps in Afghanistan and Pakistan in the early Spring of 1995. These Bosnians along with Arab "Afghans" deployed to Bosnia-Herzegovina for both operations in the Balkans as well as, should the need arise, operations in Western Europe (specifically France, the UK, Italy, and Belgium). ["Afghan" is the term used to describe those fighters trained and tested in the Afghanistan civil war. Most are of Arab, North African or Pakistani origin.] High-level Arab sources in the Middle East stressed that these Bosnia-based *Mujahedin*, especially the suicide terrorists, are being organized as a new force, forming a center for operations throughout Europe. Moreover, by the Summer of 1995, the Islamist infrastructure in Bosnia-Herzegovina had already constituted the core of a new training center for European Muslims.

This alarming terrorist build-up was not lost on the European security forces. However, hampered by constraints because of political sensitivities, efforts by West European security services proved too little, too late. In early June 1995, Italian authorities arrested a dozen Algerian Islamists, some of them "Afghans", who were running a country-wide terrorism support network. This network was living off a sound base in Bosnia-Herzegovina. The exposure of this Algerian Islamist network was a major program which took a year to complete. In late June, the French security authorities arrested more than 140 Islamist terrorists, mostly Algerian and Tunisian. This network was planning to unleash a wave of terrorism sponsored and controlled by Iranian intelligence that was to be presented as Algerian-motivated. Paris hoped that a wave of Islamist terrorism was prevented at the last minute because of these arrests.

But this was not to be. The new cells of Bosnia-based Islamist terrorists deployed since the Spring of 1995 have kept away from the veteran European networks and were thus not affected by the arrests. Instead, these terrorists operate in smaller networks run by the Iranian service, VEVAK, which relies on combat-hardened and thoroughly vetted Afghanistan and Bosnia veterans. The operatives themselves, mostly European Muslims, deploy from Bosnia-Herzegovina at the last minute. In June, such a small detachment of Algerian "Afghans" deployed from Bosnia to Paris in order to assassinate "enemies" of Islamist causes, escalate the Islamist drive into Europe, and "punish the French Government" for its support for the Algerian Government.

The still unfolding spate of bombings in Paris, as of late July 1995 was the beginning of the Islamist surge into Europe. In a September 23 communiqué released in Cairo, GIA [Algeria's Armed Islamic Group] leader Abu Abderrahman Amin explained that the bombing campaign was part of "our holy struggle and military strikes, and this time in the heart of France and its largest cities, to prove that nothing will stand in our way as long as our actions are for the sake of Allah". He stressed that the ultimate objective of the terrorism campaign was to confront the French Government so that "Islam will enter France".

By now, there was no doubt that the recent bombings in Paris were but the beginning of a new wave of Islamist terrorism in Western Europe, the work of locally-based networks deriving their support from installations in Bosnia-Herzegovina.

Although these acts of Islamist terrorism are aimed primarily to serve the long-term objectives of Iran, Sudan, and their allies in the Islamic *bloc* and are presented as being motivated by localized causes (Algeria, Palestine, etc.), Sarajevo is far from being an unwilling party or even a passive player in this Islamist terrorist offensive. Back in 1992, when the initial build-up of Islamist terrorist infrastructure was completed in Bosnia-Herzegovina, Sarajevo had already clarified its rôle in the endeavor. Sarajevo is convinced that the war in Bosnia-Herzegovina is the primary catalyst of the Islamist *jihad* in and against Western Europe. Moreover, the Bosnian Muslims have repeatedly threatened to use terrorism against Western targets if their demands were not met. Most reliable was the threat made in late January 1993 by Sefer Halilović, then the Commander in Chief of the Bosnian Army: "If Europe does not change its attitude, we will take steps and unleash terrorist actions on its territories. Many European capitals will be ablaze."

Meanwhile, European Muslim leaders continue to stress that the "absolute priority" of the Islamists of Western Europe is "participation in the fighting of the Muslims of Bosnia-Herzegovina". As the still growing Islamist terrorist infrastructure in Western Europe demonstrates, Tehran and its allies are already well underway to incite and exploit the Bosnia-Herzegovina factor in order to further their designs for an escalation of their *jihad* in Western Europe.

The growing influence of the situation in Bosnia-Herzegovina, including the reverberation of the spirit of the *fatwa*, are already felt in various Islamist communities all over the world, even in such tolerant places as London. The Declaration published in mid-August 1995 by *Hizb al-Tahrir*, the key Islamist organization in Britain, rejects the notion of a Muslim community being a part of a modern liberal state. "Muslims do not believe in integration ... Muslims must continue to present their Islamic identity therefore the only reference point for Muslims is the *Shari'ah* (divine law based upon the Qur'an and the *Sunnah* of the Prophet). In fact we are Muslims in Britain and we are not British Muslims."

In contrast, the Declaration stresses that the Muslim community in the UK should, and does, consider itself part of the world-wide Islamist struggle. "The victories, struggles, success or pain of all Muslims globally are those of the Muslims in Britain and will continue to motivate the Muslims here to strive for success in liberating occupied Muslim lands such as Kashmir, Chechnya, Palestine and Bosnia and for the establishment of the Islamic State (*Khilafah*) in the Muslims' lands." As such, *Hizb al-Tahrir* decrees, the various *fatwa*s issued by appropriate and legitimate Islamist authorities concerning the waging of *jihad* and similar issues apply to the Muslims in the UK even if they are not affected by these struggles directly. *Hizb al-Tahrir* recognizes the authority of NIF.

In late August, with a distinctly pro-Sarajevo US peace plan being pushed on the former Yugoslavia, Sarajevo's staunch Islamist supporters expressed their opinion concerning the peace process as a whole. The highest Islamist legal and ideological authorities continue to issue background material to their followers so they can better understand the NIF's position over a peaceful solution in Bosnia as well as relations between Muslims and the modern Western state.

The Islamist leadership rejects off-hand any peaceful solution for the Bosnia crisis involving the UN and the key Western powers (specifically the US, the UK, and France) because of their inherent hatred of Islam. A background study on the UN and the new world order stresses the emerging threat to the Muslims of Bosnia, and, ultimately, to the entire Muslim world. Significantly, the authors of this study sign under the group pen-name *Shehadah* which means both "Testimony" and "Martyrdom".

The Islamists insist that the UN has become an instrument of US foreign policy, and that the US is using the UN as a vehicle to impose a new international law that legitimizes crimes against Muslims including "[allowing] the Serbs to commit the ongoing genocide in Bosnia and preventing the Muslims from the basic right to defend themselves". The study warns against expecting anything from the members of the Security Council because "America, Britain and France are nothing but rabid wolves, savage beasts and conquering states". The only viable way to deal with the West is, the study warns, by confrontation.

Having rejected the present world order as inherently anti-Muslim, the *Shehadah* authors call for the establishment of an alternative, Muslim-dominated, world order. They are fully aware that this is a tall order that is not likely to be implemented anytime soon. Therefore, as practical instructions, they urge the Islamists to embark on an all-out confrontation with the US-led West until the pan-Islamic dream is realized. The Islamist leadership decrees that "this kind of confrontation with the US is not only possible but it is a must. It is not an option but a necessity, because the more we surrender to the will of the US and any colonial power the higher will be the price which we pay. We are not going to be saved if we surrender, nor are we going to get our rights by bagging the US. The US does not want to share anything with anyone, even its allies, so either we fight for our rights or we accept to give up everything and live like slaves."

Another major document issued by the highest Islamist legal and ideological authorities is a judgment decree issued by Sayyid Muhammad Qutb one of the leading Egyptian Islamist thinkers who was executed in 1965. Qutb is especially renowned for his milestone judgment decrees concerning the relationship between the believer and modern secular state (both in the Muslim world and in the West). Most important is Qutb's identification of the modern state as *Jahiliyyah* — barbarity — against which Muslims are obliged to fight.

By late August 1995, the NIF leadership was reviving the call for the implementation of Qutb's call to arms against the *Jahiliyyah*, particularly in the modern states where large Muslim communities are presently obligated to live under non-Muslim or secular regimes. Qutb's judgment decree, which the NIF leadership decrees to be both valid and timely, leaves little doubt as to what has to be done:

"It is not the function of Islam to compromise with the concepts of *Jahiliyyah* which are current in the world or to co-exist in the same land together with a *jahili* system. This was not the case when it first appeared in the world, nor will it be today or in the future. *Jahiliyyah*, to whatever period it belongs, is *Jahiliyyah*; that is, deviation from the worship of One Allah and the way of life prescribed by Allah."

According to Qutb, a political entity can be identified and defined as *Jahiliyyah* by its striving to legislate and enforce man-decreed laws: "*Jahiliyyah* is the worship of some people by others; that is to say, some people become dominant and make laws for others, regardless of whether these laws are against Allah's injunctions and without caring for the use or misuse of their authority." Thus, any secular modern state that enacts its own laws is by definition a *Jahiliyyah*. By that definition, the Sarajevo regime the US/UN peace plan is trying to impose on Bosnia-Herzegovina already falls within the definition of *Jahilliyah*, and is therefore unacceptable.

Qutb decreed, and NIF presently concurs, that there can be no co-existence between Muslims and *jahili* authorities or a *jahili* system. "Islam cannot accept any mixing with *Jahiliyyah*. Either Islam will remain, or *Jahiliyyah*; no half-half situation is possible." Qutb saw no alternative to an all out armed struggle to free the Believers from servitude to the *jahiliyyah*. "The foremost duty of Islam is to depose *Jahiliyyah* from the leadership of man, with the intention of raising human beings to that high position which Allah has chosen for him."

Significantly, Qutb used as a religious and legal precedent for the obligation to fight against *Jahiliyyah* the case of the Muslim-Arab armies' march on Persia. The armed struggle against the *Jahiliyyah*, Qutb decreed, "is explained by Rabai Bin Amer, when he replied to the Commander in Chief of the Persian army, Rustum. Rustum asked: 'For what purpose have you come?' Rabai answered: 'Allah has sent us to bring anyone who wishes from servitude to men into the service of Allah alone, from the narrowness of this world into the vastness of this world and the Hereafter, from the tyranny of religions into the justice of Islam.'"

In its present connotations, this example used by Qutb is most important to the understanding of the position of the NIF's highest Islamist legal and ideological authorities. Qutb's example and precedent can be interpreted as a justification and legitimization of active intervention by Islamists from other countries, including the use of arms, in the removal by force of a *jahili* system or *jahili* authorities off the backs of the local Believers. In modern terms: the Laws of Islam permit and demand Islamist "volunteers" to join the ranks of local Islamist terrorist and subversive groups to fight against the local state authorities. This decree also applies to the overthrowing of sinful Arab governments (Egypt, Algeria, etc.), destroying oppressive non-Muslim governments (Israel, India, and a future "secular government" in Sarajevo as demanded by the West), as well as punishing the Western enemies of Islam (US, UK, France, etc.) through the use of international terrorism. As a theologically driven organization, the NIF has the right and obligation to participate in this sacred world-wide struggle against *Jahiliyyah*. "The foremost duty of Islam is to depose *Jahiliyyah* from the leadership of man," Qutb decreed and the NIF concurs.

9. Manipulating Washington

Just as it is emerging as the springboard for anti-Western Islamist militancy, the Izetbegović administration in Sarajevo shows no inclination of giving up easily on the possibility of a US-led Western massive military intervention in the Bosnia-Herzegovina civil war. The Sarajevo regime is most interested in NATO delivering massive air strikes against the Serbs. Such an air campaign will serve Sarajevo's ultimate objective of establishing Muslim control over the entire territory of Bosnia-Herzegovina.

But Sarajevo is sufficiently realistic to know that Western Europe is increasingly reluctant to establish a Muslim state in Europe. The near-term and attainable objective is to revive in the US and Western Europe the emotional sympathy toward the suffering of Bosnian Muslim women and children: the ubiquitous victims of Serb ethnic cleansing and atrocities. As the war unfolds, Sarajevo identifies a dire need to strengthen and solidify supportive public opinion — which is fueled by emotion wrenching images rather than solid factual presentation and analysis — in order to restrain Western governments from drastically changing their Balkan policies.

Sarajevo is fully aware that as the true character of its policy, strategy and war aims — including sponsorship of and participation in Islamist international terrorism at the heart of Europe — becomes apparent, Western Governments will pause to re-examine their policies. It is therefore of crucial importance for Sarajevo to generate domestic pressure in the West which will restrain governments' ability to follow facts alone. Sarajevo's primary instrument in this strategy is the UN, because of the dominant rôle of the US — specifically Ambassador Madeleine Albright — in New York.

Hence the Bosnian Muslim strategy in the Fall of 1994, and especially in the early Summer of 1995. Back in the Fall of 1994, in the aftermath of the crisis in Sarajevo, the Bosnian Muslim government tried once again to instigate a US intervention. At the very least, Sarajevo sought to transform UNPROFOR into a distinctly pro-Muslim force. Sarajevo's supporters in the US and NATO began pushing for replacing UNPROFOR with a militarily-effective fighting force which would explicitly take sides in the war. The proponents of the idea sought a NATO task force that will take on and defeat the Serbs.

The Bosnian Muslim military strategy was optimized to serve such a move. Most important were the Bosnian Muslim offensives in Sarajevo — the center of world media attention — first in the Autumn of 1994 and again in the Spring of 1995 which were designed to compel the West to escalate its direct military intervention in order to save the innocent civilians trapped in Sarajevo. Indeed, by the early Summer this objective was realized with the establishment and initial deployment of the UN's Rapid Reaction Force to keep the road to Sarajevo open and in so doing consolidate the Bosnian Muslim hold over the city. This move formally established UNPROFOR as having explicitly and officially taken sides with the Bosnian Muslims against the Serbs. This is a fundamental transformation of the rôle of the UN from a neutral peacekeeping entity to becoming a body empowered to, and entrusted with, saving and consolidating the Sarajevo regime.

The time was ripe by the Summer of 1995 for Sarajevo to capitalize on the change in the UN's posture and make it irreversible. Sarajevo's objective is to ensure that any future peaceful and diplomatic solution to the war falling short of imposing the Bosnian Muslim regime on the Christian majority in Bosnia-Herzegovina would be politically inconceivable in the West. Therefore, the Bosnian Muslim forces launched a series of provocation offensives out of the safe areas in eastern Bosnia-Herzegovina, as well as key strategic spots in central Bosnia-Herzegovina. The military logic behind the latter attacks was to stretch Serb lines and distribution of forces.

The key offensives have been designed to create humanitarian disasters — particularly in Srebrenica and Zepa — which would induce and compel the West to intervene. These offensives constitute major gambles with the lives and wellbeing of the innocent Muslim civilian population in order to generate US/Western support as well as ensure the continued demonization of the Serbs. Sarajevo's calculations have proven correct: irrespective of the true nature of the war, the fact is that the well-armed and numerically vastly superior Bosnian Muslim forces are on the offensive all over Bosnia-Herzegovina; that the initial Bosnian Muslim attacks were launched *through* UN lines (with the Muslim forces killing and wounding the Dutch peacekeepers in Srebrenica in the process); and the images of defenseless Muslim refugees dominate Washington's policy formulation and decisionmaking. Indeed, the US is trying to generate air strikes against the Serbs which can only help the Bosnian Muslim offensives.

Sarajevo is determined to keep the humanitarian issue alive through the airing by Western media of the lingering impact of the "self-abuse" by the Izetbegović leadership of civilians in Sarajevo. The Bosnian Muslim regime is abusing its own population by denial of food (convoy blocking by breaking agreements with the Serbs and UNPROFOR) and water (refusing to utilize the water purification factory donated by the US philanthropist George Soros), all the way to the periodic self-inflicted terrorism as means of generating Western sympathy and support. The Western preoccupation with Sarajevo is diverting attention from Sarajevo's growing military might and instigating Western military intervention ranging from wider

NATO aerial bombings (which had already happened) to outright military operations with massive forces (which the US is pushing the UN and NATO into undertaking). Sarajevo is so successful because the mounting outcries in the West "to do something" in Bosnia-Herzegovina are based on emotional reaction to the increased number of images of a few civilian casualties and unproven allegations of atrocities.

However, Sarajevo no longer anticipates a major or strategic outcome of the Western intervention, if one comes. In the Summer of 1995, with hopes of a massive intervention fading because of the US-*versus*-Europe policy issue, there began a new phase in the evolution of Bosnian Muslim strategy. Militarily, Sarajevo intends to use its numerical superiority in order to launch a series of offensives developing into protracted clashes of attrition. These clashes, Sarajevo is convinced, will compel Bosnian Serb and Croat forces onto the defensive. At this point, Sarajevo believes, Washington will rally the West into imposing on the attrited and exhausted Bosnian Serbs and Croats, through both political pressure and the use of force: a political solution adverse to their vital interests.

10. Between Belgrade and Zagreb

The Bosnian Muslim grand designs were not ignored by the local powers. Fearing the horrendous ramifications of a surge of Bosnian Muslim militancy, let alone consolidation of political and territorial gains by force of arms, the Croatian leadership in Zagreb is determined to transform the war — and its inevitable and quite imminent resolution — back into its original Serb-*versus*-Croat character. Hence, faced with the possible empowerment of the Bosnian Muslims by massive US military assistance (trainers, intelligence, and weapons), Zagreb seriously studied, in the Fall of 1994, the possibility of flaring up the Krajina. Zagreb believed that such an attack would immediately regionalize the Serb-*versus*-Croat war, making it a clear confrontation between Zagreb and the Yugoslav leadership in Belgrade.

The mere existence of such a wide war throughout the former Yugoslavia would then compel the world to recognize any agreement between Zagreb and Belgrade as the sole viable option for ending the new Balkan war before it became a wider European war. In such an agreement, Zagreb was convinced, Sarajevo would disappear as a political entity.

Senior officials in both Zagreb and Belgrade are aware of this, essentially still valid, scenario. As of the Fall of 1994, they were so determined to prevent the rise of a viable Bosnian Muslim entity in Sarajevo, that they are resigned to the specter of an essentially useless and needless Serb-Croat War as the only means of compelling Europe and particularly the US to accept the destiny of the peoples of the former Yugoslavia as they desire it to be.

In mid-January 1995, Zagreb took significant steps which strongly suggested it was determined to quickly reach a settlement with Belgrade over the future of the former Yugoslavia, even if the road to such a resolution would necessitate the realization of Zagreb's own worst-case scenario: an all-out war with Serbia.

By the Spring of 1995, the Krajina issue no longer dominated Zagreb's regional policy. Determined as it remained to the objective of recovering the Serbian-held territory, Zagreb was painfully aware of the looming long-term threat of the Islamicization of Bosnia-Herzegovina. Therefore, Zagreb realized that beyond the presently-burning Krajina issue, it has common long-term interests with Belgrade. However, the lingering existence of the Krajina issue continued to drive the Croats to confrontation with the Serbs. The ramifications of this situation were most adverse in Bosnia-Herzegovina where the artificial bi-polarization of the conflict (largely because of Western/US pressure) put the Croats alongside the Bosnian Muslims whom they fear and hate, and against the Serbs with whom they would like to reach a strategic solution.

This complex and self-contradictory web of interests cannot but yield ambiguous, confused and confusing policy from Zagreb. In early May 1995, Croatia launched a "limited offensive" to destroy the Serb-held Pakrac pocket in Western Slavonia: a lightening offensive followed by the eviction of the Serb population (ethnic cleansing and atrocities included). However, this Croat offensive in Slavonia was immediately followed by a major gesture toward Belgrade, the opening of the Zagreb-Belgrade Highway No. 70 (which passes through the destroyed pocket) not only as a sign of normalization of relations between

Croatia and Yugoslavia/Serbia, but also an instrument of breaking sanctions against Yugoslavia via Croatia. But then, virtually immediately, Zagreb moved to revive the threat of a major war with Yugoslavia/Serbia. In the Summer of 1995, fearing no alternative to the cataclysmic war, Zagreb revived its claims that JNA troops and generals were involved in the Krajina and Bihac. The meaning of these claims was that any eruption of fighting, even if localized, would be considered by Zagreb to be directed against Belgrade.

However, these signals were misunderstood in the West, and especially by the Clinton Administration. Instead of realizing the extent of Zagreb's determination to re-transform the crisis in the former Yugoslavia into a bi-polar confrontation for which there is a political outcome, Washington saw in Zagreb's assertive militancy a golden instrument to "punish the Serbs" and humiliate Milošević, thus making him more vulnerable to US pressure. Therefore, as the Croatian military preparations for a major offensive progressed, Washington tacitly encouraged Zagreb to go for an all-out offensive to completely destroy the Krajina Serbs. At the same time, Washington pressured and enticed Belgrade to acquiesce to the destruction of brethren Serbs in the Krajina in return for vague political promises which the Clinton Administration never had any intention of fulfilling, and in the face of real military threats against the new Yugoslavia.

In July-August 1995, encouraged into action by Washington and Bonn, Zagreb decided to initiate the drastic altering of the situation in the former Yugoslavia. Zagreb's instrument of choice was a ruthless offensive against the Krajina Serbs. Within a few days, the massive Croat forces destroyed the Krajina as Krajina Serb forces virtually collapsed, presenting little resistance. The Croats then sent about a quarter of a million Serb refugees fleeing into northern Bosnia and Serbia, the largest population dislocation of the wars in the former Yugoslavia, and significantly larger than the entire ethnic cleansing against Muslims altogether. The far-reaching ramifications of the Croat offensives comes not from the devastating rout of the Krajina Serbs, but from the conditions prior to the beginning of the offensive. The Croat offensive was launched with the foreknowledge and tacit blessing of Washington; circumstances which overshadowed all other considerations for a more vigorous reaction from other Serb forces.

Because of these circumstances — Washington's clear endorsement of the Croat onslaught — Belgrade was deterred from interfering beyond some symbolic troop movements within Yugoslavia's borders. Consequently, Belgrade not only abandoned the Krajina Serbs who had trusted them, but shattered the overall belief in Serb unity, as well as overall Serb morale and resolve. Belgrade's inaction was the outcome of intense deliberations.

Belgrade is, late in 1995, torn between the lure of *realpolitik* and ideological commitment and responsibility to all Serbs. Belgrade's reading of *realpolitik* is that the removal of the Krajina issue from the table (even if in such a drastic form) would create the circumstances for a meaningful *rapprochement* between Zagreb and Belgrade, leading to the joint consolidation of a Serbia-Croatia condominium over, and at the expense of, Sarajevo.

But Zagreb would not let Belgrade off the hook. When the growing use of Croatian Armed Forces in offensives against the Bosnian Serbs failed to incite the Yugoslav Armed Forces to intervene in the war, Zagreb created an implied threat to a vital interest of Yugoslavia: the strategic port and airport facilities in Tivat. Using the excuse of Serb artillery fire on Dubrovnik, itself provoked by Croatian shelling, Croatia concentrated large forces in the area in late August. Fully aware of Zagreb's real intentions, Belgrade warned that recent Croat military activities around Dubrovnik suggested that Croatia "might try to draw Yugoslavia into a war around the port of Dubrovnik". And although senior Yugoslav officers stressed that Belgrade was urging restraint even in the face of massive destruction wrought upon their Serbian brethren just across the border, it is clear in Belgrade that Zagreb was pushing for an escalation.

Moreover, under US pressure to build pressure on the Bosnian Serbs, the Croatian forces, along with freshly resupplied Bosnian-Muslim forces, began preparing for a two-prong offensive on Banja Luka. The specter of such a major escalation looms ahead because all key players consider the offensive a panacea for their present strategic deadlock. Zagreb is convinced that a devastating defeat of the Bosnian Serbs such as the loss of western Bosnia would finally bring the JNA to the battleground. Washington is convinced that with a still-restrained Milošević, the defeated Bosnian Serbs will be forced to accept the horrendous and discriminatory "peace plan". Sarajevo is convinced that such an offensive would cause Serbs and Croats to attrite themselves, leaving the field open for a US-imposed solution in which the Izetbegović regime is forced upon a "unified" Bosnia-Herzegovina.

Meanwhile, Belgrade cannot erase the negative consequences of its failure to live up to the ideological expectations of saving the Krajina Serbs at virtually any cost. The weakness and hesitation demonstrated by Belgrade left a strong impression of overall Serb vulnerability among friends and foes alike; an impression which no pragmatic commitment to a long-term political solution is bound to erase.

Just as all major power centers involved in the Yugoslavia crisis were resigning themselves to the notion that the Serb-Croat solution was inevitable, the Serb self-imposed military and morale weakness, far more than the Croat resolve and might, revived Croat, Muslim and US hopes that it might still be possible to defeat the Serbs. Therefore, the Serb defeat in the Krajina which was supposed to lead to a Serb-Croat compromise ended up serving as an encouragement for the Muslims, and even the Croats, to continue and rely on the military option in order to vastly improve their strategic positions.

The place where the apparent Serb vulnerability and lack of resolve might be effectively exploited is Kosovo. Until recently, the lingering fear of inevitable and ruthless Serb reaction to any encroachment of their hallowed grounds in Kosovo served as a restraining factor for all Islamist factions striving to liberate the Albanians of Kosovo, let alone capitalize on their plight in order to escalate and widen the war against the Serbs. Presently, however, the mere existence of Kosovo as a potentially unresolved issue serves as a catalyst for a growing crisis engulfing the entire Albanian population of the Balkans. The core of the Albanian issue is the growing Islamicization of the Kosovo problem. This, in turn, enhances the potential of exploiting militant Islamism against not only Yugoslavia but also secular and increasingly Westernized Albania, as well as Macedonia. Because of the presence of US forces and diplomats, the destabilization of Albania by the Islamists emerges as an ideal way of dragging the US into active participation in the Balkan wars even if the Bosnia-Herzegovina crisis is resolved or is no longer considered valid international-political justification for such an intervention.

11. The Summer of 1995

The specter of a revived regional war directly involving the two local powers — Croatia and (the new) Yugoslavia — has returned to dominate the current dynamics. The Balkans are thus on the verge of a turning point, a dramatic breakout. All major players — that is, the local powers, the Europeans and the international players (the US and Iran) — are fully aware of the situation and the gravity of the impending event.

Both Zagreb and Belgrade are determined to bring about a situation which would compel the Europeans, and perhaps even the US, to acquiesce to a peaceful settlement between Croats and Serbs (at the expense of the Bosnian Muslims) even if such a settlement included carving up Bosnia-Herzegovina along with other changes of current borders. Despite its stunning victory at the Krajina, Zagreb is still pessimistic, convinced that only a cataclysmic Serbo-Croat war will bring about such a change. Amazingly, Belgrade remains optimistic, still hoping that a daring diplomatic initiative might still prevent the bloodshed. Belgrade still hopes that the Serbian defeat in the Krajina will create conducive conditions for negotiations with Zagreb over the carving up of Bosnia. Reluctant to get involved in a major escalation, as well as increasingly fearful of Sarajevo and its US support, the Europeans are inclined to support a peaceful settlement between Zagreb and Belgrade.

Sarajevo, fully aware of this dynamics, is determined to prevent it at all costs. Instigating a major escalation in the fighting in Bosnia-Herzegovina, especially drawing in UN/US forces to saving it, is Sarajevo's preferable method. The Bosnian Muslims are convinced that such an intervention would create a political/diplomatic situation in which key Western countries became committed (if only by the mere deployment of forces to the battlefield) to the existence of a Muslim Bosnia-Herzegovina in present borders.

Washington is at the very least supportive of Sarajevo's schemes to prevent any Belgrade-Zagreb Agreement. The Europeans (mainly French, British and German governments) are convinced that the Clinton Administration is in all likelihood the brains and power behind Sarajevo's schemes, and that Sarajevo would not have dared risk its lifeline via Croatia without US guarantees and encouragement. Moreover, the Europeans are concerned by the growing Islamist militancy of Sarajevo and the *Mujahedin* terrorist infrastructure in Bosnia-Herzegovina because these have a direct and negative impact on the stability of the Muslim émigré communities in Western Europe, not to speak of the ramifications of the bombings in Paris.

It is clear that the Europeans have a vested interest in suppressing Sarajevo. Furthermore, the European powers have religious and historic sentiments and attachments to the Serbs and Croats (not to speak of Russian-Serb solidarity), and these historic roots and legacy increasingly affect the present day policies toward Zagreb and Belgrade. Thus, the emergence of a peaceful settlement between the Serbs and Croats increasingly appeals to the Europeans even if the US is adamantly against it (perhaps *because* the US is against it).

But even if historically doomed to fail, Washington's commitment to Sarajevo cannot be ignored. Consequently, the other, albeit presently increasingly remote, specter hanging over the Balkans — a massive military intervention by US-led NATO forces against the Serbs — cannot be ignored either. Sarajevo is still making a tremendous effort to exploit its latest provocations in the safe areas and Sarajevo as excuses and justification for such a development. The US-led NATO bombing unleashed on August 30, unprecedented in its magnitude and ferocity, still fell short of the Bosnian Muslims' objective: the deployment of massive ground forces (both Western and Muslim forces) to fight on their side. If Sarajevo is successful, the ensuing escalation might turn out to be the start of a new world war. Moreover, such an intervention will deliver the spark which the Islamists are waiting for.

Even the current feverish US effort to push through a peace plan is exploited by Sarajevo as an instigation for a wider war. In late August, Sarajevo introduced Izetbegović's 12 Point Peace Plan, a document intentionally written so as not to be accepted by the Serbs under any circumstances. *With the US providing tacit support for the plan, there is no reason why Sarajevo should compromise on its extremist position.* Instead, Sarajevo issued an ultimatum to Washington. Bosnian Foreign Minister Muhamed Sacirbey told US Secretary of State Christopher that Sarajevo would give the US peace initiative only two months to make progress. If nothing tangible happened, the Muslims would commit themselves to a military solution to the conflict. Sarajevo believes that it would be possible to get UNPROFOR and NATO forces to then join the fighting in order to "compel the Serbs to accept peace" on Sarajevo's conditions.

Egypt's President Mubarak alluded to the Bosnian designs when he rejected an offensive rôle for the Egyptian forces with UNPROFOR. "They are forces to keep peace. They are not forces to fight and recapture lands," Mubarak explained.

However, Sarajevo remains convinced that the US would create for it the favorable conditions for an escalation of the war. Since the early Spring of 1995, Sarajevo and Zagreb have concluded that the Clinton Administration is so committed to the Sarajevo solution that it might decide to unilaterally intervene on behalf of the Bosnian Muslim forces for "humanitarian reasons"; using air power to save Gorazde, for example. The NATO bombing campaign launched in late August 1995 ostensibly to avenge the "Serbian mortar shell" clearly proves the accuracy of Sarajevo's calculations and planning.

Amazingly, but not surprisingly, even the massive US-led bombing and the tacit support for the Croatian-led offensives, do not diminish the the Islamists' virulent hostility to the United States. Fully aware of the crucial importance of the Islamist forces to its military capabilities, Sarajevo is not inclined to challenge them. On September 17, the *Mujahedin* Brigade spearheaded the main Bosnian Muslim offensive to lift the three-year Serb siege off the Muslim city of Maglaj. This was the only major victory gained by Muslim forces on their own.

On September 23, 1995, Abu Al-Ma'ali, the commander and "Ameer" of the *Mujahedin* Brigade, issued a report to the NIF leadership on the strategic importance and ramifications of the then still unfolding offensive. "It was a great victory for Allah indeed," Abu Al-Ma'ali wrote. He warned against losing sight of the real essence of the latest victories considering that "the enemies of Allah are trying to use this victory to their advantage, by announcing NATO strikes and advertising an American decision to lift the embargo against Bosnia." The Muslims must remind "these enemies" — the US and the West — "where have you been in the past four years? ... And why were you surprised to see the victory of Muslims?"

Abu Al-Ma'ali analyzes the current offensive in the context of the Christian-Western "relentless drive to control the world". The reason for the US military intervention against the Bosnian Serbs "is well-known: the US which controls this ailing world along with the Jews and Christians who hated to see the *Muwahideen* [Worshippers of one God, Muslims] becoming victorious over the worshippers of the cross, the Orthodox, and they wanted to use this [Muslim victory] for their own advantage." He ridicules the "claim that *Mujahedin* in Bosnia-Herzegovina are fighting in coordination with Americans and with the Croats. How strange!" He even calls on the leadership to educate the Muslim World that the Islamist struggle in Bosnia-Herzegovina had nothing to do with, and it had not gained from, the recent US bombing. He urges all Muslims "to be wary of the lying media, and the fabricated news, and urge them to get the news from its authentic sources".

Citing the religious-ideological sermons recently delivered in the *Mujahedin* Brigade, Abu Al-Ma'ali stressed that it was inconceivable that the Islamist forces would ever cooperate in a meaningful way with Croat, Serb, or Western forces. "We know that we will have a day in which to fight the Jews, and the Almighty will grant us victory, and also we know that the best soldiers will fight the Christians and all of these are promises and rejoices from the Messenger of Allah. So why do you think that victory would not come to Muslims from Allah. We do not believe in worshipping anyone but Allah, we disbelieved in the US and its allies, we disbelieved in transgressors and their religion which they invented and we have relied only on Allah."

Abu Al-Ma'ali reaffirms that the *Mujahedin* "are continuing on our path, until Allah opens the way from us with those unbelievers," so that the Islamist victory could be completed.

It did not take long for Abu Al-Ma'ali to clarify what he meant. On September 27, 1995, the *Mujahedin* Brigade issued an Urgent Communiqué called "European *Mujahedin* Call to Muslims!", which amounts to a call for a worldwide *jihad*:

> "To all of you Muslims of the world we send you our greetings carrying the scents of victory and the joy of *Mujahedin* so that you share with us the victories of Muslims and their power under the banner of blessed *Jihad*.
>
> "To all of you Muslims of the world we send you our appeal which we have repeated and are still repeating: TO RISE UP IN SUPPORT OF YOUR BROTHERS, and remove the obstacles [to the rule of Islam] from around you.
>
> "We send you our greetings in this victory despite the plots of the enemies and the unbelievers in an evil attempt to suppress these successes and conquests in order to claim it for themselves.
>
> "These attempts are led by the US and the Crusade West, so be aware of the plots of the enemies of Allah and their hate of Islam and Muslims, and Allah is well aware of what they do."

Thus, in this communiqué, the commander of the *Mujahedin* Brigade cited his forces' recent victories as proof that Muslims all over the world, and especially in the West, must further escalate the *jihad* against the West. He points out that the *Mujahedin's* contribution to recent victories would give the Islamists additional "power". The Islamists feel a sense of urgency because of the commonly-accepted belief that it was the US-led NATO bombing and the ensuing Croat offensive which defeated the Bosnian Serbs, and they warn about the ramifications of such beliefs. Therefore, it was imperative to escalate and expand the *jihad* wherever Muslims dwelled, and especially in Europe, in order to leave no doubt that the militant Islamist cause was dominant and triumphant.

As discussed above, Sarajevo both shares this world view and the fear of a Croat-Serb conspiracy against the Bosnian Muslims. Although the recent events — the US-led bombing and the Croat-dominated offensives — hurt the Bosnian Serb military capabilities, they did not improve Sarajevo's strategic posture. On the contrary, the presence of Croat forces in Bosnia-Herzegovina has been legitimized without Sarajevo's consent, and the size of territory they hold has increased markedly. Little wonder, therefore, that Sarajevo is increasingly concerned over the specter of a Croat-Serb anti-Muslim conspiracy inspired and sanctioned by the US. However, this innevitable clash need not prevent Sarajevo from manipulating the Clinton Administration to bomb the Serbs for them.

As predicted by Sarajevo for several months after mid-1995, the implementation of what can only be described as the US-Iranian strategy will initially prevent the cessation of the violence in the former Yugoslavia and the consolidation of a stable, if tense, Serbian-Croatian condominium. Sarajevo is convinced that rhetoric notwithstanding, the Clinton Administration will soon "succumb" to Congressional pressure and unilaterally lift the embargo to enable the Bosnian Muslims to withstand Serb-Croat onslaught. Sarajevo plans to ultimately seize the initiative and realize Delić's strategy of "liberating all Bosnian territory" by force of arms.

Even the signing of the ceasefire agreement on October 12,

1995, did not reduce the threat of expanding military operations. The emergence of a peace process — the US-sponsored New York negotiations — did not diminish either Sarajevo's desire for further escalation of the fighting against the Serbs in order to attain its maximum objectives through the use of force, or Zagreb's firm belief in the primacy of the military situation for long-term regional stability.

Sarajevo, in late 1995, was the local power most committed to a major escalation of the war. "One of the illusions of this war is that it is possible to bring this conflict to an end exclusively by political means," explained a Sarajevo intellectual very close to Izetbegović. In late September, Prime Minister Haris Silajdzić also stressed Sarajevo's commitment to the military solution. He explained that Sarajevo was "still having problems that can only be solved by military means", and that in the absence of a permanent solution in place, "our army has the task of reconquering every square centimeter of our country. ... Our army should continue the liberation of our country until an agreement has been concluded." Indeed, only a few hours after the October 12 ceasefire went into effect, Sarajevo had already accused the Bosnian Serbs of a major offensive along the key axis leading in the direction of Banja Luka. Responding to this alleged offensive enabled the 5th Corps to resume its advance.

Sarajevo was fully aware that although the Bosnian Serbs were shocked by the extent of their battlefield defeats, they still had a formidable military force and there was a limit to their ability to absorb losses. Moreover, an integral part of the US-sponsored agreement was recognition of a Bosnian Serb entity with special and legitimate relations with Yugoslavia. Therefore, within this framework, any attempt to destroy the Bosnian Serb entity, as advocated by Sarajevo, was bound to finally bring Yugoslavia into the Bosnia-Herzegovina conflict. Thus, looking at the present situation in Bosnia-Herzegovina, Sarajevo concentrates on a military confrontation with Yugoslavia as a viable objective.

For Sarajevo, the key national strategic issue is the mere

existence of the Yugoslav Army (JNA) as a viable force. Despite the bite of sanctions the JNA is still a formidable force. Sarajevo now argues that the mere existence of a JNA committed to Serb national interests constitutes a viable and lingering threat to its ability to consolidate its hold over the entire territory of Bosnia-Herzegovina: that is, over the reluctant Bosnian Serb population.

Therefore, the JNA issue must be addressed as an integral part of the Bosnia-Herzegovina long-term settlement. Clearly speaking for Izetbegović, the Sarajevo intellectual stressed that "peace in the Balkans and Bosnia cannot be achieved through negotiations if the former JNA remains a military force of regional importance. To break it and reduce its power, military assets are necessary [goals] rather than political ones," the present negotiations notwithstanding. Sarajevo is adamant that only "through military defeat it [the JNA] must be reduced to the strength of just one of the Balkan armies, [so that it] will not threaten others with its huge military apparatus, and will have no hegemonic plans".

For its part, Zagreb is also looking at improved warfighting capabilities for the major clash in and over the Bosnian territory. Presently, however, there is also increased preoccupation with a strategic balance of power through ballistic missiles and weapons of mass destruction. Indeed, an early October 1995 Croat strategic study stresses the preponderance of strategic weapons and a regional balance of power.

According to this study, Zagreb anticipates a major change in the character of the regional military dynamics. "The basic characteristic of the war conducted so far in the territories of Croatia and Bosnia-Herzegovina (except the NATO air strikes) is that it has been a conflict of a low technological level, with the application of archaic tactics, also including putting cities under siege." Croat experts are convinced that any future regional conflagration will rapidly escalate to a major mobile war with a massive use of long-range artillery, air power and even various missiles. Meeting the needs of such a war dominates the Croatian growing military build-up.

Looking further, the study points out that in the absence of "an extended peace settlement in the area", the primary challenge facing Zagreb will be "some kind of arms race between so-called Yugoslavia and Croatia", the region's leading powers. Zagreb has a clear idea as to the essence of this arms race. The study expects "attempts of both Yugoslavia and Croatia to introduce surface-to-surface missiles with a 400-kilometer range, armed with conventional warheads, with the capability of carrying chemical weapons, into their arsenals". In addition, the strategic arsenals of both sides will be reinforced with the acquisition of modern strike aircraft and smart munitions, as well as modern long-range artillery. The study also does not rule out that both Croatia and Yugoslavia will ultimately have to embark on military nuclear programs.

According to the Croatian strategic study, the primary site of future Croatia-Yugoslav contention will come from the "area of Bosnia-Herzegovina . . . taken by the Serb entity [and used] as a possible military training ground for some new threat to Croatia". This perception of the future regional war starts from a conflagration along this Yugoslav-Croatian border. There is no Bosnian entity in the recent Croat strategic study. This preoccupation with bilateral relations — Serbs *versus* Croats — fits closely with Zagreb's vision of the former Yugoslavia divided between a Croatia and a Serbia. Indeed, back in May 1995, when asked about his assessment of the region a decade from now, Tudjman himself drew a map splitting Bosnia-Herzegovina between Croatia and Serbia. Significantly, the areas in both the Krajina and western Bosnia-Herzegovina occupied by Croat forces since the Summer of 1995, as well as the primary objectives of a future offensive, closely fit with Tudjman's map.

This Croatian perception of the destiny of the former Yugoslavia is contradictory to the quintessence of the present US policy: to consolidate a viable Bosnia-Herzegovina under Izetbegović. Moreover, the dominant local powers — both Croats and Serbs — are not likely to give up on what they consider their vital interests and manifest destinies.

The Clinton Administration's Balkans policy will ultimately and inevitably fail simply because the policies pursued are contrary to the long-term historic and geo-strategic dynamics. Left to be resolved is the extent of the price the world — primarily the Western World (including the US itself) — will have to pay for the present US short-sightedness.

The unilateral official lifting of the embargo on the Bosnian Muslims — an embargo which is essentially non-existent considering the flow of arms through Croatia — will only give Moscow the formal excuse to lift the embargo on the Serbs, and permit the Germans to markedly increase their already massive military help to the Croats. Moreover, such a surge of military supplies to both Serbs and Croats will come at a time when both Zagreb and Belgrade will find themselves compelled to markedly escalate the war despite their inherent reluctance to do so.

12. Between Moscow and Bonn

The global and lasting significance of these developments can be understood only in the context of the long-term developments in both Germany and Russia. Ultimately, the future of Yugoslavia is in the hands of Bonn and Moscow: the truly dominant powers in the region.

Germany is fast becoming the dominant power in Europe, rediscovering and reviving its chauvinism and demons. The élite of both the "old Germany", and particularly the "young Germany", are convinced that the key to the future of Germany lies in looking eastward. The disappointment of the dreams of a European unity recognizing German dominance has led to the marked revival of eastern politics. A new Rapallo, preferably with France as a secondary player so that Britain and the US are isolated and hurt, is now perceived as the best course for the unified Germany. The élite of the "old Germany" seeks to economically confront and contain the US and Japan, while the élite of the "young Germany" also dislike the United States and are intensely hostile to Western political and economic ideals.

Significantly, it is the younger élite of Germany — a myriad of ideologies stretching from the extreme left, including the Greens, to the extreme right, including "establishment" neo-fascist — who strongly believe in the return to the East. For them, Germany's heritage and manifest destiny cannot flourish or be realized within the confines of a Western democracy. They revive the ideas of Ernst Niekisch as a guiding light. "Germany will not recover unless it supports in Europe a Russian-Asian thrust/upsurge," Niekisch wrote in 1930. It is this vision of the future of Germany fulcrum of an anti-Western, particularly anti-Anglo-Saxon, strategic and economic *bloc* encompassing the Euro-Asian heartlands which drives German grand strategy. In the immediate future, the primary challenge is to consolidate and cement the German-Russian hegemony over central and eastern Europe, thus creating the Euro-Asian *bloc* which would challenge the West for world primacy.

Russia sees its future in Slavic revivalism and the realization of its historic mission, the relentless drive into the Orient. Moscow is convinced that this resurgence cannot be realized, at least in the foreseeable future, but through an alliance with an assertive Germany over shared hegemony in Europe. For Moscow, the paramount global strategic development is the consolidation of Russo-Islamic hegemonic "understanding" and "co-existence" in which Moscow is both the dominant power but also recognizes the special rôle of Tehran's Islamic *bloc* in the heart of Asia but not in Europe. Since 1992, this strategy has been defined under the concept of Eurasianism [Yevrazist].

Eurasianism is a rejuvenated trend in Russian historical thought and historiography which provides the historical foundations and support for Moscow's grand strategy. Lev Nikolayevich Gumilev, one of its leading advocates, emphasizes that the history of Russ, its rise to global prominence, was characterized by "an ancient union, a union of the Slavs and the Turkic steppes", which "was founded on mutual respect and not assimilation or absorption". Leading local politicians and intellectuals in Muslim Central Asia support Eurasianism as an outlet that reconciles and permits both their aspirations for a pan-Islamic empire and the continued acquiescence to Russian hegemony. There should be no doubt as to the ultimate strategic objective of this historic trend. Indeed, Georgian leaders acknowledged in early 1992: "Russia and the Muslim World are natural allies since they both oppose the West."

The complex relations between Moscow and Tehran remain the key to the viability and success of the Eurasianism strategy. There has been a major development in Russian-Iranian relations as of the Spring of 1995, when Iran committed itself to seek a closer strategic alliance with Russia (an elaboration of the alliance consolidated in the Fall of 1987). Tehran made this fateful decision as a result of its reading of both the regional posture and domestic dynamics. Moreover, its Iranian Revolutionary Guard Corps (IRGC) High Command wants Iran to reformulate its military doctrine, de-Americanizing it and modelling it largely after the Russian Art of War. Iran is therefore committed to signing long-term political, military and economic agreements with Russia, ranging from working toward switching the entire arsenal from US to Russian armaments to the construction of several nuclear reactors.

In mid-May 1995, a high level Iranian team headed by Hassan Rouhani, an influential cleric who serves as the National Defense Council's secretary-general and vice-chairman, visited Moscow to put the finishing touches on the strategic alliance. Russia conditioned its wholehearted cooperation on Iran's support for, or at least silence about, Russia's suppression of Chechnya and the growing military involvement in Tajikistan and northern Afghanistan. Moscow warned the visiting Iranians that lack of Tehran's cooperation would significantly harm their joint objective of blocking US and Turkish hegemony in the Caucasus and Central Asia. The Russian-Iranian strategic cooperation was upgraded significantly in mid-July 1995 with the signing of a comprehensive agreement for intelligence cooperation. The agreement stressed close cooperation in regional activities in return for Iranian restraint in Chechnya. Indeed, Iran has since kept largely quiet about, and refrained from massive military aid to, the Islamist forces in Chechnya, even at the height of the crisis.

Little wonder, therefore, that Moscow is convinced that once a credible strategic posture emerges in the former Yugoslavia it would be able "to deliver" Tehran.

Thus, the only power capable of containing the Islamic *bloc* in the case of the destruction of a Muslim Bosnia is Russia. Using strategic incentives, Moscow will direct the rage and wrath of Tehran and the Islamists against the West — both Western Europe and the US — and away from central Europe. Moreover, appropriate economic and technological "incentives" from Germany will be most effective in further pacifying Iran.

Ultimately, Bonn and Moscow see in the emergence of their joint Euro-Asian *bloc* the key to their future grand strategic and economic upsurge. This is their manifest destiny in the post-Cold War world. Presently, the only event which prevents the rapid consolidation of this *bloc* is the fierce confrontation of their close protégés — the Croats and Serbs — in the former Yugoslavia. Neither Moscow nor Bonn can afford to let their protégés lose. Nor can they afford to let this fratricidal struggle continue for too long, let alone get out of hand, and delay their long-term strategic designs. United in their anti-West fervor, both Berlin and Moscow will therefore compel their protégés to reach an agreement and establish a tenuous co-existence, thus consolidating a strategic posture in Europe in which the United States will be the primary loser.

13. What Next?

The escalatory potential of the war in Bosnia-Herzegovina into a European War, and even a World War is a direct by-product of the huge strategic stakes which Russia, Germany, and the Iran-led Islamists have in the regional dynamics as contrasted by the US's reckless use of force. Thus, even a limited and localized escalation involving Western NATO forces against the Serbs, and particularly if US ground forces take part, might be sufficient a catalyst to escalate the war in Bosnia-Herzegovina beyond control. Immersed in a fierce nationalistic revival, Russia will not be able to withstand the crushing of the Serbs by a combination of NATO forces, the US and the Islamists. The Russians will intervene and tilt the scale for the Serbs, and, by default, against the Croats. This, in turn, will bring the Croats as well as their German and East European allies into the war. By now, the US will have railroaded Western Europe, through NATO, into joining the war against the Serbs.

The Croats consider the rise of militant Islam a threat greater than a Serbian ascension. Similarly, Germany dreads the consolidation of US hegemony in the Balkans. Thus, the war in the former Yugoslavia will escalate into a series of fierce clashes between the three sides and their supporting patrons.

Ultimately, after a brief yet intense war, the Russians and Germans will find themselves in a tenuous alliance to preserve their gains in Serbia and Croatia respectively. Their shared manifest destiny — a common hold over Eastern Europe and the joint surge to the Orient — is far more important for both Bonn and Moscow than the relative position of their protégés in the Balkans. Moreover, since these protégés — the Croats and Serbs — themselves yearn for a compromise with which they can live, Moscow and Bonn have a vested interest in quickly reaching a working solution. The Bosnian Muslims will be crushed in the process, and their supporters — the US and its West European allies (other than Germany) — will be considered everybody's enemies. For the Islamists, this will be the final proof of the inherent and uncompromising anti-Islam stand of the West — thus, a justification for the marked escalation of *jihad* at the heart of the West.

By now, if the fighting throughout the former Yugoslavia continues to smolder, there exists a possibility — a realistic worst case scenario — of the wars in the former Yugoslavia instigating a new world war. Despairing at the US-led West's prevention of a genuine and lasting solution for the crisis in the former Yugoslavia, all protagonists will have brought the war home to the heart of Europe, and even to the US, through international terrorism and subversion. In Western Europe, Islamist terrorism will soon engulf the vast émigré communities, transforming the revenge of Bosnia into a large-scale popular uprising — an *intifadah* — against the Western Governments. Consequently, the inevitable spread of Islamist terrorism and violence throughout Western Europe will compel Britain and France to send forces back into the Orient to save Western Europe from the rise of militant Islam. Such a surge will in turn constitute a challenge to the vital interests of Russia, Germany, and the Trans-Asian Axis. And so, the new European War will quickly evolve into a World War in which the United States is everybody's arch enemy.

14. Lest We Forget the Former Yugoslavia

The apprehension of a catastrophic escalation and apocalyptic expansion of the war of the Balkans should not obscure the reality that the peoples of Yugoslavia are still waging an historically belated surge of religious wars. Irrespective of the global ramifications of their struggles, they remain determined to settle their historical grievances in the foreseeable future, regardless of the price.

Old Yugoslavia was fractured by a surge of quest for religious and ethno-centrist self-determination by all segments of the population. The population's ethnic zeal is clearly expressed in the horrendous "ethnic cleansing" exercised by all sides. Gradually and grudgingly, the West was willing to recognize the fracturing of Yugoslavia but only in the context of the Republics' official frontiers. However, these frontiers were originally drawn in the late-1940s by Tito's communist regime with the *specific intent* to fracture and suppress the country's nationalities so that they would not be able to mobilize and endanger Tito's central government. Special attention was paid to the castration of Serbia because of the Serbs' support for the Monarchist *Ćetniks*, and not Tito's *Partisans*, during World War II. Therefore, until there is a reconciliation between the genuine popular rejuvenation on ethno-centrist grounds and the confinement of the population to obsolete and meaningless boundaries, peace will not come to the Balkans.

The West must realize and recognize that the peoples of the former Yugoslavia are waging this historically belated surge of religious wars, and that they are determined to settle a millennia of grievances by force of arms. Presently, however, the West continues to insist on these peoples' casting aside these outbursts of fundamental emotions in the name of imposing a New World Order which is both alien to their cultures and incapable of solving their inherent problems. The imposition of simple solutions based on conventional political formulas in order to ensure a semblance of peace and stability has long been Washington's preferred solution to complex problems. Thus, with the US-led West insisting on the inviolability of Tito's map-makings, imposing sanctions and threatening military actions in the process, Yugoslavia's prostrate population would ultimately turn on the West as the cause of its agony.

Professor Stjepan G. Mestrović, a Croat-American sociologist, stressed in 1993 that the policies pursued by the West have completely ignored the realities of the Balkans and, particularly, the aspirations of the indigenous population. The continued insistence on a political solution contradictory to the local popular aspirations, and in spite of the intensity of the popular fighting to reject such a solution, Mestrović argued, makes the West responsible for the lingering war in the former Yugoslavia. "The West tried to preserve an artificial Yugoslavia for purely modernist reasons ... and to contain 'tribalism' and nationalism," Mestrović wrote. "But in the end, history won over modernist forces in the Balkans." And it is in that triumph of history, given the prevailing conditions in the former Yugoslavia as well as the long-term legacy of a bitter fratricidal war and foreign intervention, that future peril lurks.

Throughout their history, the Serbs have been the victims of oppression by big powers which have used military power to achieve their goals. The Serbs have thus seen no other way of realizing their national aspirations and gaining their freedom but through war. "If Serbia wants to live in honor, she can do so only by this war. This war is determined by our obligation to our traditions and our culture. This war derives from the duty of our race which will not permit us to be assimilated," stressed a Serb nationalist intellectual. Foreign observers have no doubt that such a Balkan war is likely to expand beyond its original confines. "Serbia may some day set Europe by the ears and bring about a universal conflict on the Continent," warned the British Ambassador. "It will be lucky if Europe succeeds in avoiding war as a result of the present crisis."

As it was, Colonel Dragutin Dimitriević Apis defined Serbia's destiny in May 1912, and Sir Fairfax Cartwright wrote his prophetic warning in January 1913. Having since gone through two European wars transformed into world wars, with the first beginning in Sarajevo (lest we forget) must the US Clinton Administration instigate and head toward a third world war?

Selected Bibliography

A Note On Sources

Offensive in the Balkans is based for the most part on extensive indigenous material from all sides involved in the fighting in the former Yugoslavia itself, as well as from Europe (including Russia), the Middle East and the Muslim World. This material includes wire-service reports by local and international news agencies; numerous articles from the local newspapers, periodicals, and newsletters; transcripts of broadcasts on the local media (mostly translated by the US Government's FBIS/JPRS); huge quantities of original source material retrieved through the Internet, as well as a private collection of several thousand books, manuals and articles. In addition, the author draws on a unique private collection of primary sources — plus original publications, documents and reports — developed over nearly two decades of intensive research. Moreover, the author had extensive interviews and communications with numerous officials, commanders, emigrés, defectors and otherwise involved individuals from all sides. This wide range of sources constitutes a unique data base for expert analysis regarding the subjects in question.

Selected Bibliography

These are the primary sources used for the writing of *Offensive in the Balkans*. They constitute but a fraction of the diverse material consulted over the years of research.

News Agencies

AFP (France)
AIM (Independent opposition service in the new Yugoslavia)
ANATOLIA (Turkey)
AP (US)
ATA (Albania)
BH PRESS (Bosnian Government)
BINA (Belgrade based, Serbian service)
DRINA (*ad hoc* Bosnian Muslim service from the pockets in eastern Bosnia)
FONET (Serbian independent service)
HABENA (Bosnian Croat organ of Herzeg-Bosna)
HINA (Croatia)
INTERFAX (Russia)
IRNA (Iran)
ISA-PRESS (Sandzak-based Islamic service close to Sarajevo)
ISKRA (Krajina Serbs)
MAKPRES (Former Yugoslav Republic of Macedonia)
MENA (Egypt)
MONTENA-FAX (Independent service in Montenegro)

Offensive in the Balkans

ONASA (Islamist service closely associated with the Bosnian Government)
Reuters (US/UK)
SIA (Serbian service)
SRNA (Bosnian Serb, the organ of the Republic of Srpska)
STA (Slovenia)
TANJUG (Yugoslavia)
TASS (USSR)
TIKER (Belgrade based independent service)
ZBIA (Abdić's organ)

Main Periodicals And Newspapers

Al-Alam (UK-based Arab)
Al-Hayah (UK-based Arab)
Al-Majalla (UK-based Arab)
Al-Sharq al-Awsat (UK-based Arab)
Al-Shira (Lebanon)
Al-Watan al-Arabi (Europe-based Arab)
Al-Wasat (UK-based Arab)
BiH Eksklusiv (Croatia, Bosnian Croats)
Bild (Germany)
Borba (Yugoslavia)
Bulvar (Turkey)
Corriere Della Sera (Italy)
Danas (Croatia)
Daily Telegraph (UK)
Sunday Telegraph (UK)
Dawn (Pakistan)
Defense & Foreign Affairs: Strategic Policy (UK/US)
Delo (Slovenia)
Der Spiegel (Germany)
Die Welt (Germany)
Dnevnik (Slovenia)
Duga (Yugoslavia)
Economist (UK)
Ekonomska Politika (Yugoslavia)
Ettela'at (Iran)
European (UK)
Financial Times (UK)
Flaka e Vellazarimit (Macedonia)
Focus (Germany)
Foreign Affairs (US)
Foreign Policy (US)
Foreign Report (UK)
Frankfurter Allgemeine Zeitung (Germany)
Glas Slavonije (Croatia, Slavonia)
Glasnik (Croatia)
Globe and Mail (Canada)
Globus (Croatia)
Guardian (UK)
Ha'Aretz (Israel)
Hrvatski Vojnik (Croatia)
Hürriyet (Turkey)
Independent (UK)
Intelligence Newsletter (France)
International Herald Tribune (France/International)
Intervju (Yugoslavia)
Izvestiya (Russia)
Jane's Defence Weekly (UK)
Jane's Intelligence Review (formerly *Jane's Soviet Intelligence Review*) (UK)
Javnost (Republic of Srpska)
Jeune Afrique (France)

Jomhuri-ye Islami (Iran)
Keyhan (UK-based Iranian opposition)
Keyhan (Iran)
Krasnaya Zvezda (Russia)
L'Evenement du Jeudi (France)
L'Express (France)
Le Figaro (France)
Le Monde (France)
Le Nouvel Observateur (France)
Le Point (France)
Los Angeles Times (US)
Ma'ariv (Israel)
Magyar Szo (Yugoslavia, Vojvodina)
Milliyet (Turkey)
Mladina (Slovenia)
Monitor (Yugoslavia, Montenegro)
Muslim (Pakistan)
Nedjeljna Dalmacija (Croatia, Dalmatia)
New York Times (US)
Nezavisimaya Gazeta (Russia)
Nimrooz (UK-based Iranian opposition)
Nin (Yugoslavia)
Nova Makedonija (Macedonia)
Novi List (Croatia)
Observer (UK)
Odbrana (Macedonia)
Oslobodjenje (Sarajevo and international edition in Slovenia)
Pobjeda (Yugoslavia, Montenegro)
Politika (Yugoslavia)
Politika Ekspress (Yugoslavia)
Puls (Macedonia)
Slobodna Dalmacija (Croatia, Dalmatia)
Slovenec (Slovenia)
Srpska Rec (Yugoslavia)
The Times and *The Sunday Times* (UK)
Tehran Times (Iran)
Telegraph and *The Sunday Telegraph* (UK)
US News & World Report (US)
Vecer (Macedonia)
Vecernje Novosti (Yugoslavia)
Vecernji List (Croatia)
Vjestnik (Croatia)
Vojska (Yugoslavia)
Voyenno Istoricheskiy Zhurnal (Russia)
Vreme (Yugoslavia)
War Report (UK)
Washington Post (US)
Washington Times (US)
Yediot Aharonot (Israel)
Zarubezhnoye Voyennye Obozreniye (Russia)

Selected Books

[R] = Russian. [F] = French

Almond, Mark. *Europe's Backyard War: The War in the Balkans*, London, Mandarin, 1994
Ansel, Walter. *Hitler and the Middle Sea*, Durham NC, Duke University Press, 1972
Baker, James A. III with DeFrank, Thomas M. *The Politics of Diplomacy: Revolution, War and Peace 1989-1992*, New York NY, G.P. Putnam's Sons, 1995
Banac, Ivo. *The National Question in Yugoslavia: Origins, History, and Politics*, Cornell PA, Cornell University Press, 1984

Bat Ye'or (ps.). *Les Chretientes d'Orient entre Jihad et Dhimmitude*, Paris, Les Editions du Cerf, 1991 [F]
Baudson, Gerard. *L'Europe des Apatrides*, Paris, Luynes, 1994 [F]
Beloff, Nora. *Tito's Flawed Legacy*, London, Gollancz, 1985
Bodansky, Yossef. *Target America: Terrorism in the US Today* [European edition as *Target the West: Terrorism in the World Today*], New York, NY, SPI Books, 1993
Bolger, Daniel P. *Savage Peace: Americans at War in the 1990s*, Novato, CA, Presidio, 1995
Cohen, Lenard J. *Broken Bonds: The Disintegration of Yugoslavia*, Boulder CO, Westeview Press, 1993
Commandant Franchet (pseudonym of a French senior officer). *Casque Bleu pour Rien: Ce que j'ai vraiment vu en Bosnie*, Paris, J. C. Lattes, 1995 [F]
Copley, Gregory R. *Defense & Foreign Affairs Handbook*, London, IMC (numerous editions)
Ćosić, Dobrica. *La Yougoslavie et la Question Serbe*, Lausane, L'Age d'Homme, 1992 [F]
Crnobrnja, Mihailo. *The Yugoslav Drama*, London, I.B.Tauris, 1994
Dedijer, Vladimir. *The Yugoslav Auschwitz and the Vatican*, Buffalo NY, Prometheus Books, 1992 (1988)
Denitch, Bogdan. *Ethnic Nationalism: The Tragic Death of Yugoslavia*, Minneapolis MN, University of Minnesota Press, 1994
Dizdarević, Zlatko. *Sarajevo: A War Journal*, New York NY, Fromm International, 1993
Dragnich, Alex N. *Serbs and Croats: The Struggle in Yugoslavia*, New York NY, Harcourt Brace Jovanovich, 1992
Foretic, Milijenko. *Dubrovnik in War*, Zagreb, Harvatska Sveucilisna Naklada, 1993
Fuller, Graham F. and Lesser, Ian O. *A Sense of Siege: The Geopolitics of Islam and the West*, Boulder, CO, Westview, 1995
Gallois, Pierre-Marie. *Le Soleil d'Allah aveugle l'Occident*, Lausanne, L'Age d'Homme, 1995 [F]
Gareyev, Gen.-Arm. Mahmut Ahmedovich. *Yesli Zavtra Voyna?*, Moscow, VlaDar, 1995 [R]
Glenny, Misha. *The Fall of Yugoslavia: The Third Balkan War*, London, Penguin Books, 1993
Gutmann, Roy. *A Witness to Genocide: The First Inside Account of the Horrors of Ethnic Cleansing in Bosnia*, Shaftesbury, Element Publishing, 1993
Harris, Paul. *Somebody Else's War: Reports from the Balkan Frontlines*, Kranj (Slovenia), Gorenjski Tisk & SPA books in the UK, 1992
Hlaic, Col. Vladimir (ed.). *Tito's Military Accomplishment*, Belgrade, Narodna Armija, 1977
Ivanović, Dr Stanoje. *The Creation and Changes of the Internal Borders of Yugoslavia*, Belgrade, Serbian Ministry of Information, n.d.
Izetbegović, Alija Ali. *Islam Between East and West*, Indianapolis, IN, American Trust Publications, 1989
Jones Christopher D. *Soviet Influence in Eastern Europe: Political Autonomy and the Warsaw Pact*, New York NY, Praeger, 1981
Kaplan, Robert D. *Balkan Ghosts: A Journey through History*, New York NY, St.Martin's Press, 1993
Laffin, John. *Holy War: Islam Fights*, London, Grafton, 1988
Lewis, Bernard and Schnapper, Dominique (eds.). *Muslims in Europe*, London, Pinter, 1994
MacKenzie, Maj.-Gen. Lewis. *Peacekeeper: The Road to Sarajevo*, Vancouver/Toronto, Douglas & McIntyre, 1993
Maclean, Fitzroy. *Eastern Approaches*, New York NY, Atheneum, 1984 (1949)
Magas, Branka. *The Destruction of Yugoslavia*, London, Verso, 1993
Martin, David. *Patriot or Traitor: The Case of General Mihailović*, Stanford CA, Hoover Inst, Press, 1978
McAdams, C. Michael. *Croatia: Myth and Reality*, Arcadia CA, CIS Monograph, 1992
Merlino, Jacques. *Les Veritez Yugoslaves ne sont pas Toutes Bonnes a Dire*, Paris, Albin Michel, 1993 [F]
Mestrović, Stjepan G. with Letica, Slaven and Goreta, Miroslav. *Habits of the Balkan Heart: Social Character and the Fall of Communism*, College Station TX, Texas A&M University Press, 1993
Micheletti, Eric & Debay, Yves. *War in the Balkans 1991-1993*, Poole, Histoire & Collections, 1993
Mojzes, Paul. *Yugoslavian Inferno: Ethnoreligious Warfare in the Balkans*, New York NY, Continuum, 1994
Norris, H.T. *Islam in the Balkans*, Columbia SC, University of South Carolina Press, 1993
Pinson, Mark (ed.). *The Muslims of Bosnia-Herzegovina*, Cambridge MA, Harvard University Press, 1994
Rakowska-Harmstone, Teresa (ed.). *Communism in Eastern Europe*, Bloomington IN, Indiana University Press, 1984
Samary, Catherine. *La Dechirure Yougoslave*, Paris, L'Harmattan, 1994 [F]
Sekelj, Laslo. *Yugoslavia: The Process of Disintegration*. New York NY, Columbia University Press, 1993
Sherman, Arnold. *Perfidity in the Balkans: The Rape of Yugoslavia*, Athens, Psichogios Publications, 1993
Stewart, Col. Bob. *Broken Lives: A Personal View of the Bosnian Conflict*, London, Harper Collins, 1993
Thompson, Mark. *A Paper House: The Ending of Yugoslavia*, New York NY, Pantheon, 1992
West, Rebecca. *Black Lamb and Grey Falcon: A Journey through Yugoslavia*, London, Penguin, 1982 (1941)
Woodward Susan L. *Balkan Tragedy: Chaos and Dissolution After the Cold War*, Washington D.C., Brookings, 1995
Zecevic, Miodrag and Lekic, Bogdan. *Frontiers and Internal Territorial Division in Yugoslavia*, Belgrade, Serbian Ministry of Information, 1991

The Author

Yossef Bodansky is Director of Research of the International Strategic Studies Association, and is also the Director of the Congressional Task Force on Terrorism and Unconventional Warfare of the US House of Representatives. He is also a contributing editor to the *Defense & Foreign Affairs* group of publications. He is the author of three books (*Target America, Terror,* and *Crisis in Korea*), as well as several book chapters, entries for the *International Military and Defense Encyclopedia*, and numerous articles in several periodicals, including *Global Affairs, Jane's Defence Weekly, Defense & Foreign Affairs Strategic Policy,* and *Business Week*.

In the 1980s, he acted as a senior consultant for the US Department of Defense and the US Department of State.

You
can participate more effectively in international policy as a member of the

International Strategic Studies Association

The International Strategic Studies Association, based in the Washington DC area, is a worldwide membership organization for professionals involved in national and international security policy and studies. It is a major forum for debate and research, and was formed to create a focus for regular discussion on strategic issues, including defense, defense industrial concerns (including defense conversion to non-defense use), international technology transfer, geopolitical and political philosophy, psychological strategy, military doctrine and operations, peacekeeping, intelligence collection and analysis, economics, history, and much more.

Join today, and receive a special subscription to the monthly **Defense & Foreign Affairs Strategic Policy** journal (a $132 value). You'll also get regular editions of **ISSA Update**, and you'll get discounts on important books and ISSA conferences and seminars worldwide. ISSA hosts regular luncheon seminars in the Washington DC area, as well as other meetings around the world.

Yes: I wish to apply for ISSA membership

☐ My US$120 Individual Membership annual dues are enclosed herewith.
☐ We wish to apply for Institutional Membership at $1,000 a year. Check enclosed.
☐ I wish to apply for ISSA Life Membership. My $1,000 is enclosed herewith.
☐ Please charge my ☐ American Express ☐ Visa ☐ MasterCard/Access ☐ Diners

Card No.:_____Exp. Date:_____

Signature: _____

Name/Title/Rank: _____

Address:_____

_____

Please indicate professional area: ☐ Military ☐ Government ☐ Industry ☐ Academia ☐ Media

Send to: Membership Committee, ISSA, PO Box 20407, Alexandria, VA 22320, USA.